The Cast of Valor

More titles of St. Augustine's Press & Dumb Ox Books

Marion Montgomery, *With Walker Percy at the Tupperware Pary*

Marion Montgomery, *Romancing Reality*

Marion Montgomery, *Making: The Proper Habit of Our Being*

Servais Pinckaers, O.P., *Morality: The Catholic View*

Ralph McInerny, *Some Catholic Writers*

Ralph McInerny, *The Soul of Wit*

Ralph McInerny, *Shakespearean Variations*

J. Bottum, *The Fall and other Poems*

Josef Pieper, *In Tune with the World: A Theory of Festivity*

Josef Pieper, *What Catholics Believe*

Josef Pieper, *Happiness and Contemplation*

Peter Kreeft, *The Philosophy of Jesus*

Peter Kreeft, *Jesus-Shock*

René Girard, *A Theater of Envy: William Shakespeare*

Robert Hugh Benson, *Lord of the World*

Kenneth D. Whitehead, ed., *The Catholic Imagination*

Florent Gaboriau, *The Conversion of Edith Stein*

Peter Geach, *God and the Soul*

Peter Augustine Lawler, *Homeless and at Home in America*

Dietrich von Hildebrand, *The Heart*

Dietrich von Hildebrand, *The Nature of Love*

Michael Davis, *The Philosophy of Poetry*

Michael Davis, *Wonderlust: Ruminations on Liberal Education*

Aristotle, *Aristotle – On Poetics*

James V. Schall, *Sum Total of Human Happiness*

Roger Scruton, *Xanthippic Dialogues*

Roger Scruton, *Perictione in Colophon*

C.S. Lewis, *The Latin Letters of C.S. Lewis*

Jacques Maritain, *Natural Law*

Rémi Brague, *Eccentric Culture*

Richard A. Watson, *Descartes's Ballet*

Charles E. Rice and Theresa Farnan, *Where Did I Come From? Where Am I Going? How Do I Get There? Straight Answers for Young Catholics*

The Cast of Valor

Rollin A. Lasseter

Introduction by Patricia Buckley Bozell

ST. AUGUSTINE'S PRESS
South Bend, Indiana
2008

Manufactured in the United States of America.

1 2 3 4 5 6   14 13 12 11 10 09 08

Library of Congress Cataloging in Publication Data
Lasseter, Rollin A., 1939-
    The cast of valor / by Rollin A. Lasseter ; introduction by Patricia Buckley Bozell.
    p. cm.
    ISBN-13: 978-1-58731-100-0 (pbk.: alk. paper)
    ISBN-10: 1-58731-100-3 (pbk.: alk. paper)
    I. Title.
PS3612.A867.C37 2008
811'.6 – dc22   2008009136

∞ The paper used in this publication meets the minimum requirements of the American National Standard for Information Sciences – Permanence of Paper for Printed Materials, ANSI Z39.48-1984.

ST. AUGUSTINE'S PRESS
www.staugustine.net

Table of Contents

IV. VISIONS OF SPACE AND TIME

V. LOVE AND MARRIAGE

VI. THE KING IN EXILE

Introduction

Patricia Buckley Bozell

15 October, 2007, St. Teresa of Avila

AT THE ONSET OF ROLLIN LASSETER'S POETIC CAREER, HIS MENTOR, the Tennessee poet Donald Davidson, wrote an introduction to Lasseter's *Flags and Other Poems* (1963); the words are true today:

> In their blend of the modern and traditional, Mr. Lasseter's poems reflect the uneasiness (and perhaps some of the weariness) of a generation that is being asked contradictorily by our society to be both skeptical and trustful. Mr. Lasseter is skeptical, yes – as some preceding generations have not been. But he is skeptical of the secular promises that our society keeps making. God's promises are another matter.

Forty-five years of meditation and creative energy since his last publication have peaked in the poetry of these pages. During those years of gestation, Dr. Rollin Lasseter was also writing critical essays, teaching literature and history to two generations of students, and advising independent Catholic schools on their classical curricula.

Dr. Lasseter, a Tennessean by birth, studied at Vanderbilt and Yale. He married Ruth Allison Davis in 1967; they have six children and eight grandchildren. Born into the Episcopal Church, he became a Catholic in 1980, and has found his church and poetic home there for the past twenty-seven years.

A deep skepticism about modern notions of progress and utopia imbue much of his poetry with the theme of exile – the exile of the modern Southern poet from his unique heritage, the exile of so many Catholics and Protestants from the truths of their traditions. Exile and loss meet in these poems in the many images of conflict, whether outright war, religious doubt, or simply grief. Loss and defeat – along with inner victory – suffuse the Confederate defeat at Nashville, the subject of a central poem, "The Cast of Valor." But perseverance through the afflictions of religious doubt ("Experiment") or the arid desert ("the Hole in Noon" in the long ode, "St. Silence") leads the poet past the tired world of conventional sophistries into the light of truth and God's love.

Cardinal Ratzinger, Pope Benedict XVI, in his retreat meditations for the Curia in 1983, wrote of that inner desert in *Journey to Easter.*

> The desert is the place of silence, of solitude. It is the absence of the exchanges of daily life . . . the desert is the place of the absolute, the place of freedom, which sets man before the ultimate demands. . . . And so this place, with its harsh burning light, appears to be the extreme opposite of life, a dangerous threatening waste.

The antidote to this desert, as Dr. Lasseter has discovered, is the recognition of the divine presence, of the sacramental nature of all things. The deepest meaning of love of family, of wife, children, siblings, friends, is fulfilled in the divine love of God for Mankind, and the human love for God by His creation. Thus, unsurprisingly, nature images, as well as historical events and family characters, fill Lasseter's works. Only this could produce, in our time, the imagined reflections of Giovanni Batista Montini, Pope Paul VI, on his historical and world-shattering encyclical *Humanae Vitae* (1968) banning birth control, as in the long dramatic monologue, "Dawn on Lateran." The concluding lines of that poem, the Pope's last thoughts, sum up well Rollin Lasseter's poetic output:

> "*Ite Missa Est.*" I can foresee my epitaph.
> Beyond the human, beyond Law and fate
> Lies mystery, Love infinite, desire.
> The mystery of suffering hides the gate
> Of Heaven, exchange of fire for fire.
> All moments one, the agony, the wait,
> The Judgment, Resurrection, and ascending gyre.
> Praise to the hands, forgot in the debate,
> That break the bread of sacrifice each day.

Introduction

I. FLAGS

FLAGS

(Iris growing on the battlefield of Nashville)

Flags, white flags among the winds,
Do you not recall that maddened spring where men were riding?
Flags, you white and purple flags,
Stiff beauty out of gnarled bulb in mud,
Do you have heirloom memory, bulb splitting from bulb,
Hoof thunder and caisson in the roads, the screams
Of battle joy? Why, immortal beauties, am I only
Caught by death shades, the long-loved time,
Dream of the cannon and rifle smoke pregnating earth
You feed on, and do die, not fluttering in the wind
In proud and power hued innocence, marked with no blood?
Or do you, flags, white flags among the winds,
Contain those ghosts, imprison in serenity of threes
Their hate, hope, fear; their fictions, loves, and joy,
And build tight triads in the wind lest time destroy?

RAIL FENCES FROM THE AIR

As if the stretches of split rail and stone
Could slice the curve of earth and close the tone
Of grass in wet morning unto one man,
They have strung,
By the accident of dead men's plan,
They have hung
In the valley webs of stick and pebble blown
By chance in vain hope to live alone.

We who from high windows watch the scene
Of valleys know no fence breaks boundaries clean –
The soil leaps to the wind to cross our lines
And the leaves
Born on trees claimed with trespass signs,
Careless leaves,
Litter the fields shut off behind a screen
Of titles and feed the unowned wild-sown bean.

This is the power of barriers, a rail
Knocked to the ground by winds or an angry hail
Mocking our efforts to mark mine and yours
By an act
For the Earth need not enter through proper doors
And the fact
Of our bounds is broken on a single nail,
Admission that time drags down the intruding rail.

4

WAR'S PROFIT:
A Minié Ball on the Brush-Grown Field

Hot sear of Autumn fading
On a frost held road
And a tree snap under relentless axe
Harbinger the bone crack and the charred heart,
The horse scream high on new Highlands
But still Gaelic shrill,
A new Culloden for the clans pipeless to pour
On the English violence beyond Scotch-Irish ken,
New violence of burst restraint
Blackening the dawn with cannon.
And the charge will come
As at Flodden, but the peace, Culloden peace,
Will pacify only the dead.

Hood One-arm riding to the muffled drum
Heard in the dawn-chill a ghost laugh soft,
Of bosom burned in imprisoning folds,
Remarking secretly fan hid –
"He was a gallant dancer, before . . ."
And felt 'gainst the horse ribs' heaving
The leap of a leg no longer his.

IGNORANCE

To know 's not worth the wish when night's moon-dark.
Trees can know nothing.
To trace, blind to the Roman salt and flame,
The ox-hide circle
Of a town with the bronze queen in her pride,
Or leap the digging,
Flaunt my twin's design despite his iron wrath:
Grass can see nothing.
God! To enrage the kings before Beziers
From pitiless zeal
And deaf my ears when the stakes vibrate from screams.
Wind can hear nothing.

I. Flags

FOR W. B. YEATS – A PROMISE

You ask me, Yeats, having asked
Yourself, to make "one poem, cold
And passionate as the dawn."
And I'll try, never having fished
A Sligo stream, or Davidson;

But I've waked up at light on hills
At Harpeth Narrows, when the frost
Grew around shrub stems in swirls.
So pardon me if I postpone the task
A year, kind Rule; I'll not forget
The rouge of brightening clouds or sweep
Of gold out of dull skies to East,
Or even kidney-stinging damp
Chill in crisp air.

         But now the moon
Contends to win my year from noon,
And confidently I'll sit down
To watch who wins, then join you soon.

STEUBENVILLE, OHIO, 1961

Who know no setting of the sun,
No settling light in grace its living done,
To whom the day's dimmed light,
    The night choked dark,
Both night and day one laboring
    In that dark,
The sun at zenith a red disk through smoke –
    blacked air
Know little at the earth beneath their feet –
The gutted hills that elsewhere would be fair
With strong grass or sly laurel grown –
And ignorant of sun-rest know
    No labor but defeat.

SOME NEW HAVEN IMPUDENCES

The darkling plain, the raven's share with wolves,
The warriors by ruined walls where the hoar-frost curls?
There's left our one last battle, thirsty one,
Not yet a full engagement, though of rout
We know too much to wonder what its end.
When on the sea-racked headlands of the West
My banner rises a blue flame in night
To summon one last rush against the foe,
Black riders.

When that horn winds loud at last,
Slicing thick mists above the sea's roaring,
And I know no waiting's left me, no time to fat
Lean frames with idleness, I'll maybe answer
If I can, the call to stand, and lose with ire.

But, hook-nose, if you plan some new defeat
Between me and that most dread battlefield,
Take care you do not lose me on the way,
An unexpected casualty in practice wars;
For if my banner's not with those that wave
Defiant love when gathering gloom descends,
Which of us two will know who finally wins?

NEW HAVEN SNOW NIGHT

Step out, proud walker, to enjoy this hush
The low, sung murmur of earth-wedding skies.
Hear the flakes fall and the ice pop, hear
And join the sacrament of silence for a time.
New England evergreen affects a stylish ice,
Bending, dark ladies tall and proud, white arms
In graceful dance of peace. Their spell is sure.
Repeat their spell, unthinking shaker; hold
Back desire to shatter for your sport their grace.
They will not sing to beauty enviers
Soft laughing songs, tree tales of leaf and bole,
Dry teaching songs, tree tragedies of Fall.
Nor can they keep their proffered peace against loud men.

Wreck only in the summer if you must;
Green grows again; it's artless and a child.
But snow is for the season of a dream;
It builds beyond the mysteries of Chartres
Its twisted vaults and buttress beyond plan.
The blanket roof we tread on hides. . . . Ah Lord!
What fantasies forbidden man?

                    The trees
Vested for winter matins know
What curls about their feet and sing in silence.
Charm is snow, a greater art than fire.
Trees love no fire. Fire breaks the fuse of Spring.
Ask then what transept falls beneath each step?
What form is outraged by a shaken branch?
Take care you know the surface, walker, where
You think you stand; observe its grace, its charms.
Revel the eye among the shifting shapes
And take your pleasure with the world that is.

After the footfall, after the unchecked reach,
The world's made new, and its changed face burns cold
Into the heart, demanding art again.
So know the surface well, snow walker. Know.
Know surface and be wise with tangible dreams.
The cold pool waits where firm snow seems.
Then when your black feet tramp their fill and tear
The white world grey, look for the dream, free walker,
Through your chosen world. The snow offered.

THE DIONYSIAN CLOUD

"Rising from the direction of Eleusis, turns across the deserted Attic plain toward the Persian Camp . . ." – Herodotus

". . . As if occasioned by some thirty thousand."
What a fool that Greek historian!
What pedantry to dare speak so of Iacchos'
Cloud as if by mortals churned, or worse
To specify how many feet might raise
That portent. Had he not Eleusis near
Enough to know those ivory feet, though two,
Stir greater madness daily than that dust?

Pity those *barbaroi* from Asia,
To hear that horrid voice first time on strange
Soil, sacred to hostile gods, burst clear
Above the Attic plain and shake the stones
Of Salamis across her doom-deep bay.
That voice had vanquished greater heroes born
Expecting some day they would hear his flute
Insane the hills, and screaming race its fade.

Enraptured sound! Such harmony to fall
To earth from chaos-torment of poor dust.
An irony to Perse, perhaps, untaught
That dust has no defense from those wild notes
And, reasonless, must dance in choral swirl,
Hiding and following the silver pipes
To find an unwarned blood to chill with fire,
A virgin ear to burst with crazed desire.

I. Flags

ODE ON THE POSSIBILITY OF THE HEROIC

Were there but time to wait or hope
For Magnus Annus or the scope
Of gods to see the ends and means,
All justified in time where queens
  Betray no kings,
  Alloy no rings,
Nor lose ancestral thrones for careless things!

Between Troy's sack and raped Berlin
Rears more than years, and trembling men
Excuse recurrent rage with names
Expediently righting flames –
  Yet, Odysseus knew
  His horse must brew
The tempests only tricks would brave him through.

If then to craft and skill our time
Would bow, must we as he then climb
Charybdis' tree, our mushroom cloud,
And brave the dark with fire for shroud?
  The wine dark sea
  In flame swept free
Of men and gods is scarce the Hellenes' lea.

  Odysseus without craft
  Builds neither horse nor raft,
  But self-unknown with unpurposed act
  Never delivers a land attacked
  By greed and lechery
  Or faithful wife sets free.

Did that mad Geat in Heorot's vault
Consider his heroic fault
Or tear the whale path with his arm
Ruminating on war's alarm?
    Wrenched Grendel's joint
    Clocked in the point
Where gods debilitate whom they anoint.

Then to a cavern's gloom unknown
Must men drag on, subject alone
To Fate, predestined to their dooms
By voices from ancestral tombs?
    The Norse coasts' fog
    Like urban smog
Obscures and amplifies a howling dog.

    The demon haunted fen
    Where phantom lights contend
    Impressed but could not slow the Geat
    Plunging two days to chance defeat
    And best the foul hag's dread –
    Knowing his gods long dead.

Did Gideon with his lamps repeat
The Hellene? or the blood mad Geat?
The blazing tents of Midianites
Stir Israel's war songs as he fights,
    And sure of God
    Whose press he trod
He slakes the blood thirst of Jezreel's clod.

Was equally assured his Lord
Of Gideon's far-reaching sword
That he from victory would return
An ephod, not for corpse-spoil burn?

And Baal o'erthrown
Would scour the stone
To burn his God incense on virgin throne?

So, turned the chosen hand,
God's gift becomes MY land;
The high groves and the fires undo
The purity that brave men woo;
And god-called heroes choose
A tyranny when they refuse.

Love, purpose, fury, will,
Coupled with timely skill,
Return the Hellene from the sea,
Wear down the fire-drake finally,
Marauding Midianite
That flame and cold blade smite.

So to resolve the past
Clean analyzed and classed,
The muse directs the pilgrim mind
Hoping the eye that looks not blind
To sparks within a fire
That ash and winters tire.

The shadow on the grass
Dissolves as bodies pass;
The leaf heel-mangled may repair
Itself, though feel that heel was there,
And bleeding in the sun
That heel and leaf are one.

THE GARDEN

Garden of artifice grown beyond sun or rain
Revels in day born full-armed from the heart.
Myriad detail of dawn delight ignores night stain;
Blossom nor bud parthenal has here an art,
Dew burnt away with spring youth in soul's Sun and Rain.

The honeybee feeds at the flower,
The beetle prates,
The furworm frozen, come not yet his hour,
Exchrysalates,
Full summer forces to unvanquished power –
The sly snail waits.

Circling of annals torment the loves of Man.
Who loved mankind died eyeless on bloody bed;
Who loved man's mind dried, mourning a bloodstained kin;
Who loved man's honour withered, high where he fled.
Love but this garden, soul, if winter would creep in.

The honeybee fades at his flower,
The beetle abates,
The furworm full-furbished come round his hour
Enchrysalates,
Old summer burns out the last fuel of power –
The sly snail waits.

DOMINE PROBASTI ME – PSALM 139

How shall I from Thy Wrath, O Lord,
Stuff my dry head rattling in the wind?
Shall I crawl deep in some damp limestone hole,
Choke down dark air and muffle the noise of war
To the slap of slick blind fish? Dear God, you'd come!
Though cloaked in Mindanao Deep's hot wave
Among the remnants of the sea-brave dead
I dive for silence, what good then? The whale laughs.
Proud princes on Atlantis' heights withdrew
In gem-crust helms to fragile solitudes.
And in Ravenna's blazing books of light
Byzantine saints stepped up to alcoves, vaults,
And altar screens, candles smoothing rude Goths.
Brick roofs and steel a mountain thick with lead
Plates stop the furious strontium count and yet
One mortar splice gives way, enough for you;
I will go down to the crowds that multitude
Macadam lawns, and in that number twist
And twine my eyes to melting shapes among
Unseeing walkers where no blood urge draws,
And with the indifferent forest trees their limbs
Sucking the Earth and drinking rain will take
The sun and pay my daily exhalation
To peer vegetables; there will be Peace.
But if that last disguise fail, *Domine*, and wrath
Still follows my sore feet, where will I creep
To deaf the bare, black, bawling, burying blast of Love?

TO GOD THE SON, THE GREATEST FISHERMAN

This old hook twisted in Austin's golden flame
Derides the struggling of your bait, my Lord.
Do you think worm on any hook may tame
Its own pain and still wriggle on the cord
For fish mouths' hope? Good God, fish in the sky
For Satan, not for me. We're too small catch
For any palate, broil us, bake, or fry.
What profit to You or him in our dispatch?

Unless, God help me, I'm not bait for Earth,
But spitted on Faith's twists You dangle me
To stir up mud and boast a false-fed worth,
Shadowed in shallows of the firmer sea;
And what you fish for, who and where, still waits.
Too wary of the hook for quieter baits.

HARPETH POEMS

NOTE: In 1843, Montgomery Bell, Tennessee industrialist, caused to be carved a hundred foot tunnel through the limestone bluffs that force the Harpeth River to make a seven mile bend, ending almost where it began on the other side of the narrow bluff wall. Bell's hope was that the river, having taken a new course through his tunnel, would provide power to operate the great steel forges he there envisioned. Time and new power sources shattered his hopes for an industrial center; but the tunnel, long abandoned, remains his monument in the Harpeth Valley, where Indian mounds and Confederate entrenchments weather away under the eyes of those who climb the bluffs for the spectacular double valley of Harpeth Narrows.

DARK POOL

The dark pool in that tunnel waits,
Bell's tunnel of defiance to decrees,
Where the waters pass
With heavy glass
All weariness of motion to the seas
Of fates.

Climb down, young innocent, the path
Young laughing lovers insolently made
From the road's eyes
To the tunnel's prize,
And find with them the darkly singing shade
Of wrath.

There where each tunnel mouth is dark
The pool sleeps in her balanced solitude.
Daemonic deep
Filled high with sleep,
Dream haunted shadows writhing to elude
Your mark.

Dead men that light and beckon in
The daring watcher on the ledge's crown –
Slave and slaver faces,
Convict of all races,
Sweat, blood, or urine trapped in earthly bone
Again.

As if some battle fought above
This mound and lost to Darkness threw them here,
Waiting in tortured deep,
Static in nightmare sleep,
Warning tunnel crawlers to beware –
What of?

But do not answer, hold and stand,
And from green shadows one wild face will come,
Call you to dive his flame,
Repeating his half-lost name –
Bell – of the whip, the hammer, and the plumb
Of plan.

And in his torment read how fast
His tunnel plunges to the mountain's core
Ten thousand thousand days
As men count what betrays.
Know how his nightmare of the chisel tore
His rest.

Go to the tunnel pool and ask
The green-lit face where life begins or dies –
After the last flake falls,
Before the great plan calls,
Or when the work complete the long dream flies
The task?

What he will tell you is your own –
If you have blood enough to understand
Where heaven ends or hell
Smiles in the thirsting well,
What he has delved is his to comprehend
Alone.

Flame on the night, the chisel's fire
Tore stone for vengeance at earth's small mistake,
Carving the tunnel's length,
All muscle, will, and strength,
All sacrifice of self and slave-sweat, could not slake
Desire.

Which way lies Heaven, up or down?
The sun fired sky is cruel to the slave –

Noon rest, the water well,
No wind, the dinner bell;
No day to sweat through in the hollowed cave
Of the crown.

I, who held converse with his spell,
Now suck the marrow of a broken bone
He lost here years before.
And drinking demon lore
Breathe torch-smoke tunneling through the night the stone
Of Hell.

ALKAEIK ELEGY

Then dare You, God, to throw me from Narrows Heights,
Who stone-fed dragged me here beyond my design,
Have now my aching trunk to toy with
Racing the wind over Harpeth's serpent coil?

All these long cent'ries where You but stirred my brain
With absent minded wrist, unaware I scorched
While you forgot your stew and dallied,
I was returning to Harpeth dry in hope.

Now you turn round and finding my heart asmoke
Me rush high here above where the waters close
And spread wide dazzling deaths I gloried
Warning my youth of despair no honor cures;

And worlds I see reformed in debating airs
Elude my hand and lip there beyond cliff edge.
Where dream and hope encrust my vision
I have seen bridges and stairs spring out in space.

Inviting me unwary to step to death,
Inveigled and gulled by lies as a destiny,
The winds and sun gold trailed from receding You
Arched and enflambeaued of buttress flown from naught

On rock and river bone from the crest is broke –
Hephaestos I will see, ever limping sore
When heart desires Olympian feasting,
Fretting and foolish the forge his one fit home,

And falter feet where feasible no road sits –
Man's houses warm with comfortable wine of friends
Remembered in that stroke of heart ache
Fierce with your Galaxies fusing in dawn Joy.

I. Flags   23

I see these cedars clinging to crack grooved cliff
Athirst and twisted high, while below the stream.
Did they, high freed of comp'ny, waken
Dawn drunk to vision You, rising easterly,

And know in desperation no Jordan theirs
Of green growth summer, drinking an easy flow,
When here, dry rock though, burst that moment
Drawn out of years, out of mind, to yearnless youth?

You will not throw us down! We are clawed in rock;
Against Your breath we wait to be breathed again.
But feet have faltered this far, wary;
Free all you cedars, my Dawn, from rooting rock!

I. Flags

TO W.B.Y. – AGAIN

"A fine day for fishing, old man Yeats."
    "Come follow me to Hell."
"I'm hiking toward the narrows' gates."
    "Drink deep from the marrow's well."

No further talk in summer's heat;
He eyed me walk away.
And if or no he felt defeat
With me, I would not stay.

Highway and low way, tar and dust,
It's Patterson's Forge for me
Beyond the roar of rubber and rust
Beyond the smoke-browned tree.

Harpeth cold under sycamore
Twists there a wild hairpin.
And seven man-miles, twist and bore,
It ends where it begins.

Circling Harpeth can not pry
Its tail into its head,
For rock bluffs longing for the sky
Relinquishes no bed.

At Harpeth Narrows that man Bell
Could not abide a bend,
Drove self and slave, rock, drill, and will,
To marry start and end.

Its artifice completes the ring;
Again the Earth's a whore.
Bell turned the hammers in to sing
And bade the forges roar.

Too many leaves have fallen brown
Too deep the river's cut
Since Bell forced Nature to lie down
And play the passive slut.

The river hairpins still the bluff
A century's six feet lower;
Bell's tunnel echoes the rebuff
Of memory, no roar.

When hiking toward the Narrows, Yeats,
I carry hook and line
To fish a while and swim a while
And laugh at all design.

Ah Yeats, once at the Narrows' height,
I set by hook and line.
For who dare watch a giant's fight
Not marveling at design?

II. ANCIENT ALLIANCES

DRIVING AWAY FROM NASHVILLE

Driving away you wonder –
What could come after hills?
What will connect the Interstate and sky?
Will there be other cities?
Or do those out there live
Beyond the sanctuary?
What tongue does the outside speak?
Have they the holy stone?
Is there the sacred stream?
Is there a Homely House
West of the Harpeth hills?

Driving away from Nashville,
All the roads lead West.
The setting sun can blind,
As evening mist descends.
Regret and shame pursue you
Transgressions of what laws?   29
Or old offenses never seen?
Just leaving is offense enough.
Exile is mortal, a Death.

You look back for one moment,
Letting road and west
Sink into dream, remembered day.
Light rolls down the bluffs
Like water after rain;
And the deep trees wake from sleep
As you name them, mile by mile:
Cedar, hemlock, tulip, pine, and oak.

Dream dawn rushes after you
Despite the evening. Certainty

Grows stronger, mile by mile,
That despite doubt, you're free.
There is a city, stone, and stream,
And there's a Homely House.
West of the Harpeth Hills,
West of the Sun and Moon.

You gun the engine,
And your road heads home.

DID YE CUM IN BY FIDDICHSIDE?

As I cam in by Fiddichside, on a May mornin',
I spied Willie MacIntosh and all his bra' boys turnin'.
Turning, burning, all the fields now churnin',
Nae more watchers ken the necht, now Auchindoun is
burnin'.

    The choking twilight spreads along the stars.
    First bird-calls break the silence of the dark;
    And in the glimmer, rustling leaves and limbs
    Betray the home-bound creatures seeking dens.
    Keep watch! Hold breath! With dawn may come your death.

    It is no world for sleep, no time to quail,
    The time for rest and solace starts to fail.
    Snap into sharp alert! No shifting posts between!
    Over the eastern hills move hosts unseen,
    Their intent, our descent, and for their cause, our end.

An' wat ye, Willie MacIntosh, an' gie ye fortune seely,
An ye would fecht a lady fair, ye mon reck her most freelie,
For burnin' and for brakin' done, ye best be makin' speedy.
Aye, burnin' Auchindoun and her, Huntley he will head ye.

    Blackbirds call out, and watchful dogs declare;
    While whiffs of smoke drift sullenly on air.
    See, there a hidden slither in the hush,
    There, furtive bursts of motion in the brush –
    The maise ablaze, and smoke-clouds mar the haze.

    Who of the faithful holds their place?
    Who holds the shield-wall in the enemy's face?
    Here in the city's suburbs no one wakes.
    The few who listen hide and suffer while heart quakes.
    Reason is prisoned and the broken Faith but treason.

O, di ye see wha's comin' fast? Or di ye see wha's here?
I spy Willie MacIntosh, and wi' him what's to fear.
Crawin', crawin', for a' your craws crawin',
They've brent your crop and tent your wing, ane hour afore
the dawnin'.

THE SPEAR, THE HAZEL, AND DIVINE HEXAMETER

I. The Delphi Road – Spear
The spear, the hazel, and divine hexameter
Meet at the world's well and are one within a word.
Up, on the hill rocks of Boeotia, a boy,
Filets of linen tied with gold coin round his brow,
Shifts to his right leg when the weak left cramps and tires.
He spies a car, some men, much bronze or gold down there.
Lest the double gulf of Corinth drink its fill
Of filial tears, the brigand's way must feed on death.
It is his moira, fortune, first loot for this life
Of brigand without city, kin, or piety
The Well-Intentioned Ones have portioned to his lot.
Such princely living for a son of kings! The road
And crime forever. He waits the car. A mortal test.
His spear against their numbers and his grieving heart.
By the Boeotian livery he knows them prey,
And by the linen bands they wear their sacred goal.
It is the god they seek, a god he knows too well.
And for disdain of gods so easily befooled,
He climbs down to the road on mutilated feet,
And insolently leans youth on the long ash spear.
Here on the dry rocks of a roadway the world's well
Showers the living in the spray of destinies.
The mocking god has prophesied, but mixed the cup
Of nightmare darkly, leaving man to separate
The spear, the hazel, in divine hexameter.

II. Rex Quondam et Futurus – Hazel
The spear, the hazel, and divine hexameter
Meet in the singing into shape of Cameleard.
Magister Merlin, on the empty plain foresees
The wreck of splendor as the magic towers rise.
Cities in waste lands, brotherhoods in hate he sings,

Holding the holy hazel stretched and true to line.
His damask cloak whips out in the cosmic wind;
And from its stars and planets, heavens join the dance.
The stones leap of themselves to hierarchies of strength
And grow to walls, roofs, towers of miracle, fantasial
Delight amid the wilderness of earth and man.
Around the point of hazel grows the darkening ring,
Plane of substantial shadow cast by conjuring.
The mage, amazed, breaks off the forming spells too late,
Catches creation's shadow with a word of power,
Sets it afloat the horizontal, and a hall
Weaves 'round it. This the seat, the Table Round of kings,
Its planar surface Unity, its sphere the Grail!
The hazel wavers, but one wave, its purpose struck
By future visioned, wreck to come. And in the stones
Themselves the flaw is laid, wherefrom the tumbling starts.
Old Merlin weeps to see his handiwork undone.
He turns to welcome back the riding king and men;
The dragon banners and the cloth of gold pass in.
And from the far horizon moves the train that bears
Toward Arthur Lancelot, and at his side the Queen.
Merlin rejects the line; his memory recalls
The spear, beside the hazel, and hexameter.

III. The Walls of Rome – Hexameter
Along the line of sight, the missile's deadly marked
Trajectory is intellect. No straightened line
But curved, in space by time, from point to waiting point,
The shortest distance of desire becomes a norm
Piercing the heart of love, the eye of light, and death.
Singing of light and darkness alternate in time.
Trajectories of shot into the dark of God –
The hole that is God, and the hole where God has been.
The walls of Rome a burden lost in time
And dimmed by history, lived out again
In song, distinguished only if at all in time

By spear, or hazel, or divine hexameter.
And to that nothing, which is everything, we point
The holy arc of power in the death-tipped line,
Not under sea but under air – which are the same,
Yet nakeder – and poise the pen to penetrate
One substance that is never there to part for us.
Thirty-two the ways of the heart, six the head,
But five the vagaries of waking sight and sound,
Contentious witnesses for men whose souls
Are barbarous, deprived of hazel's stroke and line.
The creeping creatures of the black hole spring
And know no regulation but the wield of spear –
The spear, the hazel, and divine hexameter.

THE SHIELD OF ACHILLES

She took the thing up with a tremorous hand,
Unwilling to seem eager, hopeful still,
Perhaps this toy, so new, so shiny, grand,
might yet appease, turn sorrow, turn her doom.
Behind the circuitry some hope might stay,
some time, some love, some life mortality
might spare. Her pale immortal hands might keep
of husband, son, some seasons more, before
immortal loneliness consumed her hours.

    She turned it this way, that, and to her joy
    the armament of sun, of moon, of all
    the speeding stars was there; the ways of men,
    their towns, their petty quarrels, beasts and brides,
    the growing grain, birds, trees, and long horn'd cows,
    the Ocean's wave, the rivers' runs, the mighty roll
    of universal Law were gathered there
    by invocation of design to shield
    her own, her only, who must play with war.

She thanked him who had forged it all, she shower'd
his grimed deformity with kisses
sweet, and salty from her grateful tears.

But as she gathered corselet, helm, and belt,
still shedding relieved tears, and leapt to Earth,
the gimp-legg'd smith saw mirrored in the gold
a bloody sand, a pyre, and half out-stretched,
some naked dead thing black with happy flies.

THE SACRED BLOOD OF FALLEN HEROES

I. Springs of Conflict – A *Threnodos*, After Euripides

It was a king's son herded cows,
All and alone on Ida's brows,
Piping the shepherd's songs,
Piping the love-sick songs,
Melodies stranger than fancies wild,
Like to the passionate orphic child,
Crooning the yearning Oenone taught him;
Lonely and love-starved Oenone caught him.

Then from the sleek, shining herds at pasture,
Called from the white milky herds at pasture,
Called to judge holy ladies
Choose from the jealous ladies,
Which of those goddesses call most fair?
Hera, Athene, the Foam-Born there?
Which of their offers to buy his fancy,
Kingdoms or wisdoms or woman's love? – chancy!

But when to Hellas flew Aphrodite,
Brought from her ivory house his sweetie,
Let him look in her eyes,
Portals of mysteries,
Love he gave, love he took, tossed the apple
Quick to the goddess who gave him that grapple.
Paris the shepherd boy, nowhere a match for
Helen the hungry to set her catch for!

Stasimon:

So from their joy rose war,
Hard, never yielding war;
All Hellas sails for Troy,
Over some goddess's toy,
Sword, shield, and spear to employ,
Fortunes to make at Troy.
Hurrah for war!

II. Ancient Alliances　　　　　　　　　　　　　　　　　　37

II. Presages – a *Moiralogion,* after *Iphigenia in Aulis*

But the money changer War,
Changer of young men,
Homeward from Troy will send,
Refined by fire,
A pure, perfect, shining dust
Stored in a jar.
A man's worth of ashy dust
In one little jar.

Women will wail, and the old men praise him,
Hero immortal,
Praise how he stood in the nightmare carnage,
Spear thrust around him.
But still he dies for another's woman,
Dies for a dream love.
And still she cries, for another's woman,
Lost to her lover.

How shall the grief and the anger store?
New wine, old bottles.
Muttering words and the muffled curse
On those who sent them.
How shall the sons of the House of Atreus
Come home to pleasure?
And who then will cheer them and who then
     praise them,
Lost to their lovers?

Others lie there by a broken wall,
Unknown and unsung,
Entombed in the blackened dust of Ilion,
No home for pleasure.
Handsome of limb in his beauty lies,
God-like of body,
Held down and hidden in Troy he lies,
Lost to his lover.

II. Ancient Alliances

III. Sacrifice – *Threnodos*, for Iphigenia, after Euripides

Strophe: You will be brought down from the hill-fort
Like the unblemished heifer –
Red cloaked, white necked –
And, like the silent victim's,
Cleave they your ivory throat,
As if you might their grasping hopes make good,
Assuaging the jealousy of God
O, you were not reared in your palace
To ever be drawn to the altars
By the tunes of cowherds' pipes;
Rather they nurtured you gently
There by your mother's weaving
To dance to the flutes of a royal marriage.
Safe from the jealousy of God.

Antistrophe: Look, look where the war-god creeps,
Blood where he breathes and luckless hunting.
And now here within, in the house pursuing,
Nose-ing their quarry, go the inescapable hounds.
See, see how they sniff the hallways,
Sniff at the door of the bedroom and bath.
Heavy the stink and the blood-reek draws them.
Nose-ing their quarry, go the inescapable hounds.
Hear, hear, everywhere in Hellas
Women are mourning with their during hearts
The men who left them in the war-god's pack.
Nose-ing their quarry, go the inescapable hounds.

Stasimon: Now, it will not be long
Til my smothering dream descend,
And in the dark, damp earth
I shall lie moldering.

Those that they sent to war
They know. But in place of men,
That which comes home to them
– ash in a jar.

So for now, Apollo,
Lightgod and Archer, Wolfling,
We pray, beseech, we beg, implore,
Demand, entreat, grovel, and we threaten:
Be propitious to us and to the thing we go to do!
Give to the guilty ungodliness,
And pour in our palms the gold of Troy.
Inheritance of blood! Inheritance of blood!

IV. Retribution – *Aoide: The Eumenides*, after Aeschylos

Now is the hour of the new dispensation,
No more laws, no elder godlings' order.
If this, the murder of mothers triumphs,
Nevermore will Justice' judgments shine.
Lost be the sacred blood of fallen heroes.
    Oh, how the ease of escape will impress them,
    Crime shall be open and honor mocked.
    Again and again will fall the murd'rous stroke,
    Fall on guiltless parents from their children,
    Shedding the sacred blood of fallen heroes.
Oh nevermore let the helpless victim call
On Justice to recompense for the tyrant,
Anguish and torment feeding blank despair:
Oh, Justice, come! Oh, Furies, hear me!
Gone will be blood of fallen heroes.
    So will the father wail when hope's betrayed,
    The wounded mother bleed beside her babe,
    Sorrow on sorrows crowd the smoke-filled air,
    The House of Justice falls. – forsaken, bare;
    Forgot then the sacred blood of fallen heroes.
Fear is the good, unsleeping guard of will,
Fitting it should sit before the heart's-gate,
Guarding, presiding, fiercely ordering all,
Oh, good to fear and follow wisdom.
Honoring the sacred blood of fallen heroes.
    How shall the man not trained and terror-tried
    In fear of heart – likewise a city –
    Learn and delight to live by holy law:

Praise and respect for ancient wisdom?
Mocking the sacred blood of fallen heroes?
Oh never may the wailing victim call
On Justice to defeat the bloody tyrant,
Torment and anguish only feed despair:
Oh, Justice, come! Oh, Furies, hear me!
Answer the sacred blood of fallen heroes!

SUBTERRANEAN BRACKETING

– Deuteronomy 33:27

To the tune of "Old Hundred and Twenty-Fourth" Louis
Bourgeois, 1551, [536]
"Turn Back, O Man, Foreswear thy foolish ways."

And underneath, the Everlasting Arms.
Within the shouts of victory, screams of rage,
The clangor rung on nerve by fresh alarm –
The silence of stark letters on white page:
"And underneath, the Everlasting Arms."

For past belief, the uncomplaining arms
Hold up the interlocked combatant's stage.
Clawing the backs they mount, ruthless of harm,
The companies dissolve, reform, engage
Yet underneath, the Everlasting Arms.

They fail us not, the ever-suffering arms,
Nor careless, draw us from their stage
Despite our petty sorceries and charm.
We rest enfold in comfort and in cage,
Still underneath, the Everlasting Arms.

As infants cradled in the careful arms,
So from night perils, dream's despair, the wage
Of sin, the sting of death, or war's alarms,
We sleep our little journey through the age.
And underneath, the Everlasting Arms.

II. Ancient Alliances

THE CAST OF VALOR

I. Hood in Georgia, September 16, 1864

They waited silent in the autumn rain
As it ate at hillsides raising reddening pools
Around the horses' hooves on Palmetto Plain,
Churned and grassless now that battle cools
Beneath the rain. The starved beasts scarcely strain
To crop the grass or roots left by the spavined mules
Of Georgia militia camped here in its pain
After Atlanta's burning. Terror stills
In hunger. What morning was it when a brain
Could sumph in redeye, grits, and sorghum spills
Over the plate's lip, and the smells of cane
Sugar in coffee? All lost now. Even drills
Foregone to wake the bodies fed on dream,
The Army of Tennessee put by its ills
To wait the coming of a fate those schools
Of Attica foresaw and shook that wills
Might die unto. Hood rides their lines; all, tools
To turn his destiny, with him defy the mills
Called history. Their Yell, long silent, rules
For crucifixion on the frozen hills.
Hood wheels his mare, mud splashing from the ominous pools.

II. The River Crossings, November 17, 1864

The Tennessee cut through its hills and fell
Away behind them, all now crossed, his men
Laughing away the hunger in a spell
Of ease. Hood looked upon the column's din
And heard again those voices in his hell
After the whiskey left him helpless to the grin
Of that gaping stump a leg grew on 'fore shell
Or shrapnel, either had its teeth, and he
Remembered nothing but the waking yell
Strapped to a caisson while the saw bit free
The stewmeat from his thigh. The voices well

At evenings in the damp, ancestral glee
To pull him down into the dark they dwell –
Gentleman's scorn, a baron's lust, the sea
Thick with the curraghs and the reiving kin,
And under all First Father, blood-streaked eye
Fixed on the sun that burned him, cursed his fin,
Roared at his timid progeny that wordless Me
That shook the aeons judged of rot within.
Hood heard, and as the flesh fell, Tennessee
Burst forth the pyre where God and Man at last might win.

III. Spring Hill, November 29, 1864

Could they have slept this little hour of care
And lost the victory thrown in his hands
Before? Deserted him in this, laid bare
The bulwark of his hope, surprise, for demands
Of body over will? His thought-webs tear
And sail the fields controlless. One by one his glands
Sink back to darkness in his fear and flare
Unconsorted in aimless rage. What scales
Can weigh the body's treacheries; who dare
Attempt defiance of those slowing cells?
Schofield's night-stalkers, fed and fair,
Complete their stealthy passage through exhausted spells.
Blind sentries murmur courage to the air
In hope it brings forth manna and dispels
The blur of sleep, blind eyes burning, like brands
From a redoubt burst in fire by mortar shells.
Spring Hill to shame them, and the empty lands
Taunting the starving hearts; in the cold fogs the knells
Of long dead fathers billow round the clans
Regathered on this alien field. Loss mells
Their solitude within all history's desperate stands.

IV. Franklin at Noon, November 30, 1864

"Blood stinks, Hood, and you know it, or should know
How it steams into the night. You think
By spilling more of it today you grow

Less sensible a nose? You'll barely wink
One time and to that valley's earth we'll throw
Libation of a thousand innocent throats, a drink
Hades may thirst for, but I won't." "Then go.
I'll not command you, Cheatham, to become a man.
Cleburne will rise to it. There's greater foe.
What is their wind of lead but flame to brand
Mortality on the herds of death? Where mow
The sword scythes swung by envious angels I will stand
With Jackson, Lee, or our great God of Woe
Himself, courageous, willing to demand
An end to living, if to live's to shrink
To caution and mere Right. God's moment can
Slip by us in the night; already sink
Those stars this army rose by; our shame's their van
Escaped us yestereve, now here you'd slink
Around them, poke the flank. I tell you, man
Sucks God's hind tit 'til Life is cast beyond Death's brink."

V. Franklin at Four, November 30, 1864

Banners awake and flying on the ridge,
Their snapling to the wind returns the call
Of bugle, mortal solitude down edge
Of consciousness. No Power will forestall
The lines' advance, eighteen brigades, their wedge
Slow spilling down the slopes, backs to the setting ball.
Across the valley blue boys drink the dredge
Of terror from the growing grey. The sound
Rolls on the valley, boots drummed down on sedge.
Eyes blind with death, old comrades share a round,
And hold their fire behind the bois d'arc hedge.
Toward them the rabbits bolt the grass, flushed by the pound
Of dead men moving toward this sacrilege.
As if all worlds were then in Franklin bound
Time's silence cracks as Cleburne's front ranks fall
Before exploding hell; lead winds surround
The grey lines shivering beneath the wall.
Grey men, bent forward in some dream wherein they drowned,
Breasted the wind of flame that blows us all

To night, called history by fools. So crowned
The long lines, that day, Valor with a bone-bought pall.

VI. Nashville, December 16, 1864

Down from the North and the long guns' mocking laughter
They crawl, bodies or will, whatever, broken
Back on the low hills Nashville held for after
Earthwork, trench, and Hell's guts shaken
Over their remnants worked all wills the softer
With an iron tenderness. And then to waken
To hill-ice, neutral December made a sifter
Of men and horse strength while the long guns dined
Past gluttony on raw meat. What demon-lifter
Calling in the North of a frozen mind
Pulls to these frozen hills this wolfish laughter?
What licks at the staring fallen, twists them with leaden wind?
What plan of a maniacal cosmic drafter?
Shapes for the depths, the husks of stiff mankind,
Grown with their blood-ice solid to the bracken
On the hills, like cedar-stumps entwined
Against the wind and drought on a cliff. Forsaken
By the flying files of men, he bends, now blind
With loss beyond despair, Hood, broken
In the icing rain, and feels the grind
Of stirrup on his ghost leg for a triumph token.

VII. Bainbridge, Alabama, Christmas, 1864

Wavering on the West he turns his eye
Over the Tennessee, the darkening wind
Driving the sleet down in the grey dawn sky.
The columns stumble in the mud and bend
Southward over the hills, night's shadows fly
Down from the ridges; Flapping despairs descend,
Death birds, on the North, and on the South the Lie
Of Satan nestles down along the heart.
"This how it ends," Hood broods, "ignominy
And nothing for this world saved, even in part,
From poverty and pride? Well, let it die.

II. Ancient Alliances

There is enough of glory even in devil's art
To find us and restore all we deny.
Whatever flesh we paid, this aching smart
Of leg stump or our comrades' lives, must blend
Back into beauty and all pain depart.
For we have done what makes us men: descend
The mystery of God with obedient heart.
What was our task, though Hell itself defend,
We met with valor. Now let what may start."
Hood on his ghost leg wheels and spurs off toward his end.

KENTUCKY VOICES

I listen to Kentucky voices fall
And follow out dark windings of their way
Soft tongued through laure-lodor of the day
Eased down in long coves grey with shade, and call
Of whip-poor-will late in an evening's roll.
Night walking of small insects, taking all
The day sounds down deep into sleep.
      Yet no –
      It's like a troubled sleep,
A waking sleep where distant cries are blurred,
A sleep with more of a Kaintuck mem'ry in the word,
Of forests hot with centuries of shade
And blood, cicadas scraping a taut bow,
And flint primed for the steel; as if we heard,
Behind the soft fall of a tongue, a blade.

III. THE DAUGHTERS OF DESTRUCTION
(Darkness, Dumbness, Desolation, Death)

THE DAUGHTERS OF DESTRUCTION

Daughters of Destruction, the angelic core
Of Mtatron's children, transformation's four,
Darkness and Dumbness, Desolation, Death,
Grope toward finality with soundless breath.
 All that is natural feeds to their desire.
 Thus love is source, is wellspring of all art.
 And tragic always, everywhere, our heart;
 For transformation is the function of desire.
Darkness and Dumbness, Desolation, Death –
The depth of tragedy is measured by its breadth.
All nature tragic, impotent and caught,
Entangled, snared, delivered and delayed,
 Mere men and women mumble out what's played,
 Grope, fumble, grip, and grapple ought
 That stumbles by them in the darkened bay,
 And fall at last to sleep at end of day.
Darkness and Dumbness, Desolation, Death –
The Holy Sisters wait within the breath
While life feeds emptiness its heat.
Tragedy's nature longs to be complete;
 Unless the dark be lit, the dawn be broke,
 The weather change, the sleepers woke,
 All is condemned to end upon the fire.
 For transformation is the function of desire.
Alter, O Love, this everlasting clay,
Transhumanize the tragic in our fire,
Refine all ores within intensified desire
Until the tragic rise past comedy to play.
 Then shall the angels shout,
 The stars gambol about,
 The rocks shall chant old lays,
 And comets dance their praise.
And Darkness, Dumbness, Desolation, Death,
Transformed transforming, music in the breath,
Shall step forth laughing, in our love's exchange,
Humility, and Silence, Clarity, and Change.

DARKNESS
THE PERMANENCE OF SPACE
FOR ST. JOSEPH OF COPERTINO

"Le Silence éternel de ces espaces infinies m'effraie" – Pascal

I. Sorrow Grows

Sorrow grows on us, aware
Of music in the spheres.
Dry rainfall, pattering first,
Then drumming the dried heart,
'Til infinite at last
The wells of pity pour
Cacophonies of fear.

Sorrow grows on us, aware
Musicians of the spheres.
Zeus, pater! What bolt splits air,
Deafening ears to rumors
Of despair and purifying
Waves of harmony in air?

Sorrow grows, and uses care
To break old music in the spheres.
Red angels turn the domes
Of seven heavens, bronze and brass,
To rouse us. Torpid, proud

Sorrow growing on us, ware
Of music, any music, anywhere,
The darkness lesser dread
Than silence in noon glare,

Sorrow groping on us, there,
With music, culled of spheres.
The silence terrifies.

And sorrow grows on us, aware
Still, of the music of our fears.

III. The Daughters of Destruction

II. The Common Travail

Dread body of the world, my failing flesh,
Poor figure of God's only shape
Made manifest amid the
Unity of enchained atoms,
Machinery of time, the Jester
God lives out in you his fickle will.
And in your little death,
The foul decay of flesh,
Putrescence and the stink,
Again the image of Our Lord
Word-God stamped clear.
Putrescence purified by
Christ among the atoms.
Each dismembering God's
Body by God's Word
Which was and is and is to come
To no good end save one.
Did He then see who rose beyond
Three stinking days, the
Rearrangement of his cells,
Into the spiritual plant
Sprouted in corpse's seed,
What flesh it was that
Resurrection claims is
Unseen to the corporeal eye?

III. A Grain of Sand

And what of heaven, the shadow land,
Dream haunted from our sleep,
Where all is apposite *in aeternis*
Within the very spaces of our breath,
Polarity and anti-space within
An unseen molecule
Impenetrated to our sleeping hearts,
Angels of Entropy dismembering their wings,
Their time unfocused to our time:

Athwart desire within and up?
We have the dream-god for our sign;
Material cross bearing His material weight
On armbeams spanning time and our desire,
Relieving Him at cost of agony
Uplifted moments only on the
Pierced feet by the nail of Heaven,
Devastated by the weight of dream,
Moments lifted out of time
Into the shadow land.
In that course all creation flows
In on itself, all eras one,
Turbulent of trusts and tempers
In the moment of a grain of sand.

IV. To Our Lady of Long Thought

Thought steals again, as ever, to that eye
That wound us from delight with folly, back,
When years were triumphs or defeats,
Expounding symbols like hashish or hex –
All mystery, all wet desire.
Who never knew, and cannot know now
More than faith in what eyes see,
Demon or beast or goddess taken in a net
And tied with all the knots of flesh
Yet free because wound tighter by the mind,
Whose mystery? Whose wet desire?
We weary of those secrets never solved:
To know and not know
In a world aflame
What mysteries are heart-borne,
Which made solid by our stiff desire.
Her triumph marries my defeat
To get misshapen images in trance,
New mysteries, new wet desires;
Why still, beset by enemies the heart upholds,
To hear within that abstract horde, grown cold,

Persistent rumbles of the Night she praised,
The flashes lighting wide the Western skies
And then
　　The long-locked thunder of the Cross?

V. Deep Space Our Mother

　　It is not so, these infinites
You postulate beyond the breath –
All mass but sorrow loaned
The void to give it mystery.
Should we not levitate, give utterance
Our "customary shrill cries,"
And grasp at her feet
Who treads the serpent moon?
We'd know. And know beyond
All utterance the emptiness of space.
Mass would lie waste for us
And idiot-like each great concern
Roll from our eyes into the night.
O, Mother of Mothers! Sorrowing
Mysterious matter in our nerve ends;
Nowhere the permanence of space.

　　On the long streets night bound
In New Haven once, snow fell,
Snow, *sancta camissa*,
Fell modestly when we almost
Saw nakedness revealed
And stepped through stone.
Cold in the nerve ends burned; the lights
Of store signs flickering red and blue
Flickering reflectively on wet,
　　Streets fell back, and we stepped out on emptiness.
Upheld, on darkness visible,
To preserve our name.
Then snow fell and the surface held it.
And we walked its bridge relieved.

Only, behind us, in the black pools
Of our footprints, in our past,
There were windows open
On the abyss underneath.
It is not so, we know it, despite snow,
These infinites you postulate
Beyond the reach of breath.
Mass is but mother of sorrows loaned
The void that we might suffocate.

VI. Night Silence Sings

Space infinite no more is still.
Delight, in diapason, fills our veins.
Night silence sings of Him,
Space infinitely sure, and still
The light orgiastic of it rains,
Spills, over us awash in flood
Of blood pulse threading past our ears.
Space, infinite before Him still,
Delights in silent kinship with our veins.
Night's Angels! Seraphs of the Mind!
Shut fast your Doors of Pearl against
This flood after so long our drought.
Space infinite in care now spills
Incarnate harmonies on shriveled veins.
Heart, Dia! Bromia! What sloughs
Of fleshly matter in our parched brains
Are deep enough to drain us
Lest we drown in such delight?
Space, infinitely still no more,
Delights us, urging on our veins.
Fear's silences sink down
To pity for the dying stars
As visions of our kinship with their spheres
Flare heavenward from us in the windy air.
And clear, the heart's desire is answered everywhere
Space, infinite no more, instills
But light, organic, in our pains.

III. The Daughters of Destruction

DUMBNESS: ST. SILENCE – AN ODE
For Rev. John C. Gerber, C.S.C.

"At the time of the aridities of this sensory night, God makes the exchange we mentioned by withdrawing the soul from the life of the senses and placing it in that of spirit – that is, He brings it from meditation to contemplation – where the soul no longer has the power to work or meditate with its faculties on the things of God."

> – St. John of the Cross, *The Dark Night* I. 10.1

I. THE FIRST ODE: THE WINDS OF SILENCE

I.

Come, O Saint Silence, to this crackling earth,
Come and bring Spring.
Like the last blows of winter, birth
In the heart of light the urge to sing.
Silence our chirping brain, our flapping tongue,
Quiet the bubbling heart, the hissing lung,
Soften the groaning flesh, the blood's raw rush
And on the mocking loins lay thy mute hush.
Over the avaricious eye draw shades of snow,
Blizzard the landscape in one eye-dazzling glow.
Come and bring Spring.

"Spiritual persons suffer considerable affliction in this night, owing not so much to the aridities they undergo as to their fear of having gone astray. Since they do not find support or satisfaction in good things, they believe there will be no more spiritual blessings for them and that God has abandoned them."   *The Dark Night* I.10.1

II.

Come, Lady Silence, and be seen,
Silence like gold.

Hard-edged is silence, clear and keen;
Shadows deepen and the light is bold,
Not blued like summer twilight when day's done,
But white like noon day under April sun:
Stolid as cloud-climbs on the distant sky,
Stark as the tree limbs' crisscrossed ply,
Stabile as stonework wind has worried dry,
Static as sunlight bathing the awakened eye.
Silence like gold.

"They then grow weary and strive, as was their custom, to concentrate their faculties with some satisfaction upon a subject of meditation, and they think that if they do not do this and are unaware of their activity, they are doing nothing. This effort of theirs is accompanied by an interior reluctance and repugnance on the part of the soul, for it would be pleased to dwell in that quietude and idleness without working with the faculties."   – *The Dark Night* I.10.1

III.

Come, Mistress Silence, and becalm the storms.
Come as the cold.
Out of the April noonlight, out of the forms,
Falls silence clinging to each new leaf's mold.
Mastered the marveling mind, the outraged intellect,
Sharpened our love that it may reject
Tolerant drowsing and demand our best,
Discipline wonder, and destroy the jest.
White, mid the clamorous appetites of April's noon,
There hangs, in marmoreal stillness, the day-dimmed moon.
Come, Silence cold.

"They consequently impair God's work and do not profit by their own. In searching for spirit, they lose the spirit which was the source of their tranquility and peace. They are like someone who turns from what has already been done in order to do it again, or one who leaves a city only to re-enter it, or they are like the hunter who abandons his prey to go hunting again. It is useless then for the soul to try to meditate, because it will no longer profit by this exercise."

– The Dark Night I.10.1

II. THE SECOND ODE: HOLE IN NOON

"If there is no one to understand these persons, they either turn back and abandon the road or lose courage."

– The Dark Night I.10.2

1. Blest quiet falls upon the tongue,
    Speech not allowed.
    Only the startled mind hears music sung
    Behind the ear, not loud.
    So Holy Silence silences our noise.
    Amid the rush of produce, without sign,
    Unlooked for, unexplained, when gain employs
    Our faculties to voice some grand design,
    Thou, Silence, gift of God,
    Steal'st God.
    And we are left, a moment, in our pain,
    To catch again
    That fading music without sound
    Deep in the ground.
    Not all our exercise of brain and lung
    May move the silenced tongue
    Cloven to mouth's roof.
    Proof, aloof,
    For proof is not a boon,
    Of that impatient Presence waiting in the hole in noon.

"Or at least they hinder their own progress because of their excessive diligence in treading the path of discursive meditation. They fatigue and overwork themselves, thinking that they are failing because of their negligences or sins."

– The Dark Night I.10.2

2. The blown accompaniment to silence
   Complicates the brain.
   A thousand voices crying
   To be heard above the pain;
   Thought within thought, light within light,
   A fever to explain, speak all at once the Name
   Unnameable, the Void,
   Multimaleable singularity of Word,
   Pressing to gain a tongue
   Cloven to mouth's roof,
   Proof, aloof,
   For proof is not a boon,
   Of that rich plenitude that pours from out the hole in noon.

"Meditation is now useless for them, because God is conducting them along another road, which is contemplation and which is very different from the first. For the one road belongs to discursive meditation and the other is beyond the range of the imagination and discursive reflection"

– *The Dark Night* I.10.2

3. And out of noon there opens, still,
   Nothing. Emptiness. Despair.
   The grass bends under foot; the air
   Stinks of the tailpipes racing by;
   The roofs of tenements below the hill
   Claw up and over one another for the sky –
   There are no golden domes or spires,
   No young lambs bound,
   No transformation of the ground
   Beneath the scuffed shoes of shame.
   There's just New Haven, still the same,
   Yet changed,
   Disarranged,
   Not City, but a scramble of desires.
   It is the lack of vision out of noon,
   Too soon,

That cleaves tongue to the mouth's roof.
Proof, aloof,
For proof is not a boon,
Of that disenchantment spreading out the hole in noon.

"Those who are in this situation should feel comforted; they ought to persevere patiently and not be afflicted. Let them trust in God Who does not fail those who seek Him with a simple and righteous heart."   – *The Dark Night* I. 10.3

4.   Not in the sky nor under earth that hole,
     But in broad day it stole
     A child at play under my Southern sun.
     The green world multiplying in its mortal run
     Around him, and he saw
     Withdraw
     The certainties of safety and of law.
     He saw him naked, under eye
     Of beasts and men.
     No way to fend
     The steady stealing of the soul
     Past all that natural whole.
     Awakened in the dance,
     Transhumanizing Chance,
     Circling the naked clarity of a friendly glance.
     First, then, the boy's tongue
     Clove to the mouth's roof,
     Proof, Aloof,
     For proof is not a boon,
     Of that wild providence that pulls from out the hole in noon.

"Nor does He fail to impart what is needful for the way until getting them to the clear and pure light of Love. God will give them this light by means of that other night, the night of spirit, if they merit that He place them in it."
            – *The Dark Night* I.10.3

5. Dread apparition is the light of love,
   O Lady Silence, when you come,
   Flaring across the future where we move,
   And we struck dumb.
   Old Balaam met it, who took pay
   To curse the hosts of Yah out of their way,
   In broad day,
   That unseen opposition none shall pass.
   Only his ass
   Speaking,
   Shrieking
   The promise of the Cross, a star
   From Jacob rising o'er the bar
   Of consequential law.
   Once, twice, three times his facile tongue
   Clove to the mouth's roof;
   Proof, aloof,
   For proof is not a boon,
   Of that economy that saves from out the hole in noon.

"The attitude necessary in the night of sense is to pay no
attention to discursive meditation, since this is not the time
for it."   – *The Dark Night* I. 10.4

6. Ezekiel of the exile ran
   Beside the Chebar, a new priest,
   His thirtieth year in hand.
   Looked on the fourfold Beast,
   Devoured the unclean Feast,
   Ceased
   Speaking in the tongues of Man,
   Built doll cities with his bricks and sand,
   Rolled in the mud of Babel,
   Burnt hair, ate dung,
   Still, his rebellious tongue
   Clove to the mouth's roof,
   Proof, aloof,

For proof is not a boon,
Of that wheeled Juggernaut that grinds from out the
    hole in noon.

"They should allow the soul to remain in rest and quietude, even though it may seem very obvious to them that they are doing nothing and wasting time, and even though they think this disinclination to think about anything is due to their laxity."   – *The Dark Night* I.10.4

7.   In Egypt, Jeremiah heard God swear:
     "I have laid waste your cities, sold
     Your virgin daughters for an ounce of gold.
     Your palaces are bare,
     Your hovels fare
     No grander in the ravening flame.
     And which of those your bastards care
     To name themselves by their paternal name?
     I have despoiled you, I;
     Though you may try,
     Or cry,
     To die,
     I have removed even anger's prod.
     I have abandoned you without your god."
     Cleave, tongue, to your mouth's roof –
     Proof, aloof,
     For it should be no boon,
     The emptiness of daylight spilled from out the hole in noon.

"Through patience and perseverance in prayer, they will be doing a great deal without activity on their part."
                           – *The Dark Night* I.10.4

8.   To persevere in prayer, Sweet Silence, hard
     Enough without you, harder certainly
     In certitude that prayer is stored

Against some future day.
Light rose about the incense of his Lord
To silence Zachary.
But age makes mock of such a message.
What promise left him who'd outlived his hope?
What little child might presage
Light to those in age's dark
Or shadowed in death's cope?
His laughter,
After,
Clove to the mouth's roof,
Proof, aloof, for proof's no boon,
Of that soon-given gift that grows from out the hole in noon.

"All that is required of them here is freedom of soul, that they
liberate themselves from the impediment and fatigue of ideas
and thoughts and care not about thinking and meditating."
The Dark Night I.10.4

9. Is it to teach us prayer is labor, Silence,
    That you fall,
    Turning our hymnody to sighs?
    Daylight our call.
    Ox-shouldered Thomas who had fed
    Himself and millions on the angel's bread
    Knelt on the chilling stone
    And was alone,
    Confounding councils with his interdict,
    Summations of discernment derelict,
    And tomes of argument and law
    Valued in so much straw –
    The waves of blinding light
    Clamoring against sight,
    While cloven to mouth's roof
    The proof,
    Aloof,
    For proof is not a boon,
    Of grander grammars hiding in the hole in noon.

"They must be content simply with a loving and peaceful attentiveness to God, and love without the concern, without the effort, and without the desire to taste or feel Him."

– The Dark Night I.10.4

10. Juan de la Cruz was silenced,
    Before the Dark Night was explained,
    Silenced on Virtues, when the power drained
    From his ready pen, again,
    As it had with Carmel, never to complete
    The journey's explication in iconoclastic prose.
    Only the Spiritual Song, the final Flame,
    Because they do not name
    The Nameless but repeat,
    Complete,
    The Way of Images, was he allowed to close.
    The plenitude of Image floods the brain,
    Raising the universal pain
    Beyond the strength of tongue to tell,
    Swell, to the theme of Faith, Hope, Charity.
    Tongue cleaves to the mouth's roof,
    Proof, aloof,
    For proof is not a boon,
    Of that solemnity of Love bequeathed us out the hole in
        noon.

"All these desires disquiet the soul and distract it from the peaceful quiet and sweet idleness of the contemplation which is being communicated to it."   – *The Dark Night* I.10.4

11. Old John Vianney, thought so wise
    For peasant shrewdness, at the end,
    The lines of penitents stretching round the bend,
    Found in his tongue-tied tries
    For Queen of France or ragged hag
    Only the one Word, from his Living Lord,

"Little children, love one another,"
Like his ancient brother,
Patmos-bound, when revelation dries.
Cloven to mouth's roof,
Proof,
Aloof,
For proof must not be boon,
Of that compassionate release that frees us out the hole
  in noon.

"The more a person seeks some support in knowledge and
affection the more will the soul feel its lack, for this cannot be
supplied through these sensory means."
  – *The Dark Night* I. 10.5:

12. The mysteries of Silence gather friends
  Before the final harvest ends;
  And on a hillside among wind-dried grass,
  New Haven harrowings of sight
  Opened in Autumn entry for the ghosts to pass,
  Calling each to each,
  To reach,
  Teach
  What, called or not called, answers in the night
  That all is right,
  Sin is behovely, and the very dung
  Shall in its Maker's praise shine bright
  Until the babbling tongue
  Cleave to the mouth's roof.
  Proof, aloof,
  For proof is little boon,
  Of that sure calling called us all from out the hole in noon.

"Accordingly, a person should not mind if the operations of
his faculties are being lost to him, he ought to desire rather
that this be done quickly so that he may be no obstacle to the

III. The Daughters of Destruction

operation of the infused contemplation which God is bestowing that he may receive it with more peaceful plenitude and make room in his spirit for the enkindling of the love that this dark and secret contemplation bears and communicates to his soul." – *The Dark Night* I. 10. 6

13. It is to silence us and let us hear
     The music we are stilled,
     Struck dumb in the fury of the mind.
     Bitter profundities of kind
     Are proffered and instilled
     Then closed to commerce as a cave
     Of crystal wonders twined
     Beyond the craft of dwarves is sealed
     By landshift and its rooms
     Forgotten under the enraptured moon.
     So, in a holy silence, tongue
     Cleaves to the mouth's roof,
     Proof, aloof,
     For proof's a curious boon,
     Of that deep certitude imparted out the hole in noon.

"For contemplation is nothing else than a secret and peaceful and loving inflow of God, which, if not hampered, fires the soul in the spirit of love . . ." – *The Dark Night* I. 10.6

. . . CON
ANSIAS
EN
AMORES
INFLAMADA

DESOLATION: MYSTERY OF THE GARDEN

I.

Midgarth, *hortus*, garden, yard, or Earth,
Matutina, the linguists say all bloom
From the one root. It is our dearth
We suffer from, our space mere room,
Not paradise. And earth like woman bleeds.

Each season's issue of dismay infertile among weeds.
How shall this garden-earth, Good Mother, flower
Amid the images unimaging the blessed womb?
How, desolate, the abominable desert hour
Turn, *O Arca*, monthly bleeding into bloom?

As women sacrifice beneath the monthly mill
Their season of dismay, our sweating pain
Falls to the thirsting earth without our will.
We can bear nothing, nor refuse the drain
Upon our veins, *Matrona*, of unimaging blood.

Over our forms and fantasies old sufferings flood.
And no one knows it. Unaware that dream
Wrecks on the shoals of reasoning, driven sane
Before the winds of Spirit, seeking the gleam
Of image for this suffering, the Cup, the Grail of pain.

II.

Suffering is the medium, *Matrona*, of exchange.
And by the agony our sight,
The final separations, God from God, arrange
In suffering of union will to will aright.
It is a lie, *Refugium*, that Christ obeyed.

Obedience to such destiny is frayed
Beyond belief. This Cup, he named it,
Powerless to will the drink's delight,
Obedience not in him; desolation framed it.
It was surrender, comprehension, seized his sight.

The olives live in us as we in him.
The very stones cry out as we destroy
Exchange, we see and hear of them
Only their spectral mass, mere suffering derived from joy.
We see vacuity, the impotence of sight.

To transform, transubstantiate our night,
Suffering is the medium, *O Mater*, now
For exchange. The change of suffering to joy,
Sweat rivers bleeding from the brow.
The medium of exchange, *O Stella*, must destroy.

Blood is the sign, *O Virgo*, of the curse
On Adam as on Eve – that life must pass
The confines of a seasonal hearse,
Conceive in agony and bear in mass
The suffering of souls as well as flesh.

And in that suffering sacrifice itself afresh
Upon the bed, the table, floor, the mud
Of the abandoned garden and its withered grass.
Whether it pour from wound, from womb, our blood
Repeats soul's weariness, surrenders to the pass.

So if our suffering be medium, *O Filia*, of exchange
And meaningless, unimaged, to our eyes
Except so changed, in sacrifice, *Castissima*, the strange
Meeting of the God, the horrible, with our disguise,
Then what, *O Clemens*, is exchanged for what?

III.

Or who for whom? Who bears the hurt?
The multitudes of pain prohibiting our sight
Of solace in the broken bones, the whimpered cries
Bloat-bellied children offer as they die, to whose delight
The fetus salined in the womb but to our gluttonous eyes?

We look at history, *O Turris*, and despair.
The bloated bellies, sunken eyes,

Impassive in exhaustion, everywhere,
Behind barbed wire, from rotting huts and flies,
O'erwhelm the image of Exchange, make desolate

The sanctuary of the flesh with empty fate.
How in the muddy compound where the starving stare
At desolation is the image found, *Eburnia,* to try
All postulates, the icon of Exchange? O Fair!
Bright music of those tortured eyes!

We die each other's life, live each their death,
Grow strong their weakness, writhe beneath their pain.
Not millions suffering, not mass, but breath
Of just One Sufferer is all we breathe. In plain,
There's no more pain in mass than one.

One suffers, dies, and all the sum
Of suffering through time is what one mother bears.
No hurt beyond one hurt, nor brain
To pain beyond one brain. The cares
Of desolation water the dry earth in place of rain.

O Mother, in suffering the seed of love is lain,
And desert all this garden Earth until we bear –
Bear fruit, bear burdens, bear our pain –
Must we, self-prisoners, choose this dusty share
Of heavenless matter, know it profane

And desolate, abomination in our brain,
Then carry drought, as you once carried God?
In suffering the nine-fold growth of fear,
Willing our drought, shall we be awed
Into a fallow soil that may yet bear?

IV.

In mystery of suffering hid the seed of love;
Fallow, it lay enripening in dark pain.
Dark in the fiery heart's resentments strove

Rebellious pain. Desolate the stars again.
Bare day on day. Eternal silences of space

Within the stars; within the heart no trace
Of answering life; no voice to voice; all still.
Only the pain, the flesh of infants, carrion brain
From carrion flesh, less eyes, less ears, less will,
Rotting to compost round forgotten seed inane.

The mystery of suffering hides the seed of love.
Pain changes, Mother, into novas of delight,
Illumining the shadowland, the shore
Of space-flow, tides of salt-dry fright,
Of thorny waste, the desolation of desire.

In matter thingness isolates with fire.
So, luminous with lightnings breaks each dawn
Above dry desert, desolation, darkness, bright
Hope in hopelessness, and drawn
Through pain, borne suffering gestates delight.

V.

Through devious ways, Good Mother, to the founts of time
We came, to desolation and despair,
To boredom, to disdain, and mocking rhyme.
It is the point of rest in turbulent air
Around us, Nature's crown of kingship worn.

So flesh acknowledges its nature torn.
Crowning ourselves creation's crown we come
Down desert trails, *Castissima*, through nightmare
To the thorny Garden of our ancient home
And see it as it is: Love in despair.

Sic, O Mater Fidei, infidelibus,
Ora, nunc et in hora mortis nostrae.

DEATH: FAREWELL, MY FATHER

I . The Winter Garden

Where have you stepped, my father, with your silver hair
Arranged and parted for your bridal year?
I have walked out in snowfall to the lawn
You loved to pattern to a plan for life;
And overcome with whiteness I longed for dawn,
This snowchill on the brow, since you have gone,
Have left us here with that sharp sad-edged knife
That slides against the throat – its use withdrawn –
Waiting in our too-large heritage;
The fading outlines of your certain age
Bleak out beyond us. Still our souls too small,
Untempered to approve the calm your violence
Demanded for its home. Snow covers all –
The unkempt iris beds, the borderments
Of black stone, three white steps, gray pedestal –
Make you, so carefully hid, too clear. Their hints
At knowledge bring the dark that must appall,
Thrown out in anger at our littleness,
These broken borders mock our brittleness.
Where have you hidden, Father, with your silver hair
Arranged and parted for your bridal year?

II. The Darkening Hall

All now is disparate in your family's aim,
And each runs errands at his season's call.
How far my afternoons of secret game
Listening for your word in the darkening hall,
And each room stilled by shadows 'til you came
To signal that great dinner-bustling – all,
It seemed, for one hour's gathering of your name.
I know tonight mere image can not stir
What's calmed. We wait no more homecomings, Sir.

III. The Daughters of Destruction

What portrait can amend death's insult here
Where you spoke once? Grief can not light oil eyes
Or raise a painted hand. Only the fear
Of making images be you – and lies –
Throws me into this night where senses blear
With cold – our ageless Protestant disguise.
Yet cut from icons you may disappear . . .
How dare give up your image to the snow
To keep an honest dark we can not know?
Where are you watching, Father, with your silver hair
Arranged and parted for your bridal year?

III. Southern Shades

This night, Sir, we lie waste of warriors,
Your judgment gone; in siege round the mind's wall
Old wraiths from our claymore past cry out for wars
With their frozen sorrow beyond death's recall
Each time some dropping from the slave-curse mars
Their restlessness. You had no wars at all –
Snow after harvest; after day, the stars.
But jealous powers of the vanquished past
Mount up their charge; your word by death iced fast.
Hood's empty heart, who is he that could kill
Again those dead? Always his charge undone
By that death-cold ridge, night's horror rolling still
Over the heart resigned to lose the sun.
Hood's ghost a wind around our silent hill
In Nashville, only a wind, his battles run.
Now must I mold wind to your face by will?
Where chattering dead betray our honor's stance
With rusty blades, you'd know more sure defense.
Where have you sheltered, Father, with your silver hair
Arranged and parted for your bridal year?

IV. Snow Dreams

Already in your god's house I'm alone.

No sheltering there, in those vaulting spaces night
Reduplicates upon its shade with the drone
Of frosted prayers blown in the eaves of sight.
Where you knew sustenance, I'm fed on stone.
Your god reigns fearless in his ordered height
Your virtue fitted so none need atone.
But in that frozen order's found no room
For him who stands before the empty tomb.
Your death undid that order in our eyes
And pulled the temple down on our repose
Of certainty. I fear God's great surprise
Is freedom; to be nailed or numb like those
Crazed Galileans when their righteous skies
Fell tumbling at a cock-crow and the blows
Of hammers. What virtue did they see arise?
All ancient wisdoms whirl off with the dead,
And you, Sir, leave me snow dreams fever-fed.
Where are you waiting, Father, with your silver hair
Arranged and parted for your bridal year?

V. The Quickening Wind

Who spins the vortex through the freezing air?
What darkness musters her infinite rolls?
This four-square pounded earth writhes with despair
Of armies death-locked on the Western holds;
And flights of glowing shadows surge and flare,
Break loose from their timeless wars to warn the folds
Of demon wolves. The vision breaks. I swear
The cold's our ally for it leaves no way
Neither to choose nor not choose night from day.
Old snow banks sheepishly under the wind
On brown bulb rows of iris, lacking fire
To purge or prove. Snow has no foe, no friend.
Seasons obey the wind and the wind's desire
Turns quickener when the winter's bulbs distend
For spring. That breath will serve me too, inspire
Me for these foreign wars, to your same end.

I searching darkness without proof of dawn
May meet you sooner, now I know you gone.
Far from your steps, my father, and your silver hair,
We range with ghostly allies in this bridal year.

IV. VISIONS OF SPACE AND TIME

THE BUSHEL

"Neither do men light a candle and place it under a bushel."
                                                        – Matthew 5:15

I am a lamp. I am a candle, light
To the nations – of the deaf and dumb.
And He has set me, under His bushel,
Damped, dark, deprived – but not of light.
What man would light a lamp, and set
It under a bucket, or a bushel? On
A lamp-stand, maybe, on a hill, or window
For travelers to spy across the night-veiled miles.
No man, no man, and yet He covers –
Could He be waiting for a certain hour?
Could He be holding the lamp-wick safe?
Around my little bushel wall the winds
Howl in anger and try reaching in,
But the weave of wicker thwarts them.
The crystal flame glows on. The wick is safe.
As for me, waiting, I must rely on shadows,
Ancient interplay of good and wrong, His tale.
And the uncertain forms of wars without
Seen only through the wicker in dim shade,
They may be heroes, thieves, or even djinns,
But this vast bushel holds, and lasts.
I am a lamp, I am a candle, light
To straggling pilgrims on the darkened road.
He will know when to lift His bushel,
He will know when to move His hand.
It is His light I tend and wait for day.

NIGHT THOUGHTS

Night thoughts obsess the heart, and follies reign,
For wind blows dry and cold over the grass.
There is a lapse in logic for the sense.

Pondering blasphemies, he cries,
Struck to the heart by emptiness.
Slowly the stars depart the night.

There is no reason for his obloquy,
No reason for his sorrow in the night.
Dawn and nightfall are the same.

A dog barks in the evening air,
Answering other barks from round the bend.
Nature speaks out to nature in the night.

But nowhere does the wind find rest.
It circles rounded Earth seeking the east,
And only in the whirlwind finds its home.

Where is the whip-or-will? Where the thrush?
The barren limbs sink down with beating rains,
And no call answers from the darkling wood.

Wondering where the mystery descends,
Where legend slips to history and lives,
He takes his walk, and watches sand in wind.

When squirrels hide and crows cling to their perch,
When even beetles run beneath the roots,
Darkness descends, borne on the wings of storm.

Somewhere the breezes blow, somewhere the rains,
Somewhere dawn twilight grows within the eye.
Night thoughts obsess the heart and sorrows weigh.

IV. Visions of Space and Time

There is no answer in the ancient runes,
No message in the movement of the leaves,
Only the silence of the sleeping stones, and dawn.

ACEDIA, THE DEMON

It sits as one uncounted angel on
The pinpoint, refusing to be moved,
Or join the dance. How many angels can
Inhabit space without respect for dance?
That little riddle pesters, others fail.
Is Hell not dancing? Or a dream of dearth?
Ye angels of grey dawn, sound clarion!
Arise, take hands, step to the Holy Drum of Heav'n!
Sleepers, awake! Our diapasoned joy and jest
Break forth across your shadowed hills of day!
Dance, dance, ye mortal creatures to our song!
Now is the hour of mirth, the tick of sorrow, Word
And wordless spin between the flights of Hands.
Sing, sing, ye mortals, dying, living, in that dance!
It sedentates the mind to keep soul dumb
Amid the tumult of the romp, denies their joy,
Refuses sight. The Arresting Angel, stiff
With pain and poverty, resentment, rage,
Alone, turns dawn to drab within the eye.
Hell, then, the figures of the entwined souls
Frozen by fusion with the pointed pin.
Sing, therefore, soul! Sing and clasp angel hands!
Drab in the twilight dawn the promised day.
Dance, then, and weave with angel wings the sky!
Weave into precept, statute, maxim, rule
The rhythms rising from the spawn of day!
Sing out high harmonies heard deep before they fade!
Sing, dance, desire, ye mortals, precedence on the pin!
It will not raise the head. It sinks, fatigued,
Mid angels, arrogant as ever, worn
By battle with the heedless stars of fate.
Sinks to defeat. It will not dance; can't dance,
Will never dance, to music others hear.
It is the Angel of Despair, Time's Tread,
Lord of our secret lust, would wish us dead.

THE LABYRINTH

Who would then claim this labyrinth
Has warmed his April days,
That in the heat of summer night
Mocked all high thoughts we praise?

But she led right, I think,
And strung me through the maze.
Where do we go if not the length?

To grip fast sword and shield, that's all,
This darkness entered far,
Where in the dip of any floor
Waits the elusive Minotaur.

One knows the end, yet all –
Aware of what may bar
Escape, clutches the raveling ball.

DOT TO DOT

Space has no walls, no prisons for the eye.
Only unseen patterns folding in and out
Among the faces and the limbs.
And lines are constructs of the eye connecting points
Invisible, and yet seen there.
The line joins space.
The line is space.
There is nothing there,
but space,
    and points,
    and lines.
Oh gods! how empty! how inane! how vain our conjurings
To capture love!
And yet it is, this line, this jointure of invisible spots of time.
It is as love is,
There but not there,
not here, not anywhere but deep within the core,
Holding the points together, frail and wan.
It is the rope across abyss, the razor's bridge,
It is the road to everywhere. It is
Our wind-swayed love.
Beauty is real. Our eros fails to see.
Beauty is distant and the line a road.
Beauty dissolves timidity but calls us out
To walk the swaying rope-bridge of the line on empty space.

EXPERIMENT

Perilous atop the bluff, one pine
Clinging to stone with roots deep curled
Faces the winds, its branches gnarled
By age and stress to phantasms of line,

A mystery. All mysteries. All secrets of the law.
And into that dark labyrinth man's mind,
Deprived of light beyond the urge of kind,
Where only fang had pried and paw,

Poking and piercing where the hungers lead,
Tears flesh's veil and finds death stopped the flood.
Directed solely by the pulse of blood
Mind finds what eye and ear decreed.

Like to that pine the imprisoned soul again,
Bound to the rack and touched with fire,
Endures "experiment" to test desire,
And answer truth from agony and pain.

Winds of the soul, the shapers of the mind,
Surge through the pain to force from what was dark
Some truth, some hidden link that ignites spark
And turns the darkness light, though eye be blind.

Perilous atop the bluff, that pine
Clings to the stone with roots deep curled
Bends with the winds, its branches gnarled
By age and stress to curled truth in the line.

RESEARCH

Searching the darkness of the inner world,
The torturer of nature pries the truth
Out of the silent matter, tooth by tooth,
And maps the universes round him whirled.

Mysteries of atoms, molecules,
The juncture of unasked for solar planes,
The micro-universe arranged by change
Of permutation, chimes and peals,

The intersection of vibrating waves
Of heat and pitch. The music of the spheres
Aligned by human will in layers
Novel or at least untried. Time saves

From out the jumbles one or two or three,
The chance eruption of a gambled flair,
And in the heat and pressure new- made pairs
Deliver new nadir and apogee.

VISIONS OF SPACE AND TIME
For Benjamin

I. Clouds of Witness

Drawn near the central mystery of life,
You, Son, stand with us here in prayer
Where all our fathers dwell, the long exchange
Of shouldered burdens not our own; our weight,
The sums of error and regret, of hurts
Inflicted wittingly or not, all borne
In full, perfect, and sufficient sacrifice
Until His coming again. Stand with us now,
Here, in the central mystery of life.

All that this cloud of witnesses proclaim
Is ours, the vision, order, nurture, place,
As called before His Mystery we tend
The daily sacrifice of Godly will.
Alone, yet not alone, taking the food,
We draw our generations to the type:
And in the incensed shadows of the flames,
Participate this princely benefice,
All that these witnesses proclaim as ours.

Caught in the candles' flicker and the smoke,
The cloud of witnesses press in, surround.
And we, late worshipers arrived before
The transubstantial conversion
Catch glimpses of companions in the crowd,
Corporeal in some counterfolded time
Not ours, participant with us in this
The point of change, Spirit's descent to flesh,
Caught in the candles' flicker and the smoke.

II. Wood, Leaf, and Root

It is no vision now we seek, no light
Raying the heavenly throne, no dragon's roar.

Earth has dissolved for us, the fixed bounds fallen,
Houses and streets transparent to the eye
With hard derision of solidity.
That was enough. God showed Himself in Space.
It is the Company we seek, Christ's flesh,
The watchful attitude of holy life.
Living the god shown once within the world
Is constant prayer, beyond those ancient sights,
In efficacy brighter than their fear.
So we await, remade each, year by year,
Joined to the thronging shadows round the flames.
There is no vision now that speaks His Name.

Trees should be trees, wood, leaf and root.
Not ganglia, not patterns of the heart,
Not men a-walking, no, nor cruciform,
But trees, all the analogues of mind.
The oak and pine embody now all these.
And through their dancing boughs a window shows
The multifoliate reality
Of Time where earth is heaven and we are home.
In each new bud, in blossom, spring green shade,
The wonder of degree begins its climb;
And we ascend, freed of the concrete tombs
Streets, houses, monuments had made for us.
Trees are now trees, wood, leaf and root.

III. The Folds of Time

Time folds upon itself like gossamer,
All moments one and present here, distinct,
Remembered, held and lost, in symmetry,
As we surround the Meal, the bread, the wine –
Fold upon fold of Time, the veils of God.

What watchful worshipers, half-recognized,
Enshadowed, from our past, what other days

Beyond our deaths, what other worlds entire,
Stare back at us over the acts of hands,
The making and confecting priestly hands?

Who crowds with ghostly forms about the cup?
We, who were here, will be, stand even now
Tensed on the edge of Time, taste, and we see
The multifoliate reality.
Time folds upon the heart's eternity.

THE OLD ONES
For Ruth Katherine

There is a stillness underneath the trees,
A silence, as the afternoon
Lifts slowly, without sound or breeze.

Half-missed within the corner of the eye,
Dark shapes withdraw behind the rocks
And disappear under the evening sky.

There are unspotted beings there,
Behind the tree-boles hidden down
And waiting to appear in air.

They watch our clumsy cavalcade
Make merry through the fallen leaves
And listen, waiting, as our voices fade.

What do they do when we have passed?
What is their picnic in the gloom?
Or do they feed on shadows while they last?

PILGRIMAGE
For Austin

The August stillness lies along the sight,
Woods dark against the gold
Fields, hills, and clouds, each particle of light
Paused, poised, the summer's increase told –

Only the hawk's cry in the silent air,
Bird-quarrels stopped, frogs hushed, flies stunned,
Thick corn rows baking in the sun's slow glare.
We stop. The quarter-day is passed. The hunt is turned.

Over the wide-waved earth at anchorage
All airs abate. We lower to their sleep,
Sinking in silence at the pilgrimage
Of motion, through wide portals, vast and deep.

WINTERSCAPE
The Harpeth River, December

Showered by snowfalls as the branches break,
 The forest path grows dim in evening dusk.
And owls reply, deep in the gloom awake,
 Like ghostly mourners for earth's icy husk.

White over black, the snow-robed sentinels
 Cover the rushing stream, black waters roll,
Resound through dream worlds, woods and fells,
 Bewintered as the hush blankets the whole.

Like snow-wrapped boughs bend to the frozen earth
 And sip black waters rushing beneath their root,
Frozen and bowed, the wintry soul athirst
 Dips into perilous waters burbling at its foot.

What does the forest watch? What the stream see?
Frozen in silent darkness, they see me.

THE PRIMAL LIE

The Triune waited on the adamantine throne.
The Princes of the Universe rose to advise,
But nowhere could the rudiments of love be found;
So armies struggled for the mast'ry and the godheads
groaned.

And there was war in Heaven, Satan's host
Uprisen and in arms against the Throne.
Justice for all creation so engrossed
His sifting mind with measures that he shone
Against God's blackness with a flaming boast
Of wisdom weightful for that swirling question grown
Within the Throne's Eye when the worlds were tossed
Disordered out of darkness into night.
All the archangels listened, but the most
Part, those to whose care new weak worlds in flight
Were trusted, found Satan's desire less cost
To what they cared for and his rebel answer right
To end the chaos through their crashing posts.
Michaël shouted NO over the bright
Design because it came, not from the Throne,
But from that brilliance of the rival might
So long preferred as if the One condone
Its will in question and its hope another's sight.

"As merit so the meed:" Satan's alone
The gnome, and at the thought there broke First Light
Out of the Depths of Silence. And the Law was stone.

> They had expected it, who see all that is to come,
> This massacre of energies at war and who would win.
> But what they saw made nightmare of the first sure plan,
> And cast the Three in opposition to their works.

Then there was night in Heaven with the Fall
Nor any world nor angel to defy

Necessity in the concentric ball.
Darkness enthroned looked into its new eye,
By Order seeing Order within all
Its Self; and where none reigned before, now Merit's cry
Was answered and obeyed as seraphs roll
To ranks delighted at the ease their play
Among the universe now knew, and wall
On wall of reasons for the Right dismay
The exercises of the Powers' sprawl
About the spheres, until their joyous disarray
Was stilled and structured to the Law's fixed toll.
The Order ranked by virtue all that lay
Beneath the Throne and gave each rank the high
Call to surpass its Kind and climb the way
To greater virtue, so that all should vie
For precedence of Right, so striving to repay
Obediently the sight that let them fly
First into life, they strove that new lives may
Taste light each in their turn and age consent to die.

    Yet Death was not willed in plan. The Triune turned;
    Yet in the certainty of good, they let what be.
    Somewhere the final shapes of things would follow Love,
    If only war among the powers would cease.

Woe upon wavering woe convulsed the worlds
As cycles dropped away from God's intent,
Deficient in their aim; and, from the swirls
Of power terror spewed, each complement
Of angels born expanded from sleep's whirls
And vanished back again where so deemed exigent
The rule of Merit's Right. The eddying purls
Awaken, flare, and die, sparks from a fire
Upon the night.
              Rebellion grew in furls
Invisible but to its mind, and higher
Rose Michaël on each comb of burls
Out of the majesty of Crown. Satan's desire
Michael matched with rage; and downward hurls

The Dragon from the Throne he would acquire.
He rises, coils, and taunts Michaël's dissent
Unworthy and unthought. "The swallowing pyre
Of Reason is our check 'gainst ravishment
In Nature by mere whim of pure lives that aspire
Toward Light, toward Dark when usefulness is spent."
But on Michaël surged in holy ire,
And Darkness riv'n between them screamed upon assent.

    The Triune Darkness, pained by what the plan
    Demanded, yet gave way to Love, and let the free go free.

The Darkness wrinkled on the Throne, His mind
Befuddled like some gaffer's at this light
Of Satan's and the shape his Order limned
Over the deep. That death should be the plight
Of any His Creation burned His blind
Eye that he'd not foreseen that Order, working, might
Entail the orderless be undermined
By Order and displaced out of the day.
Where would the dying end?
                    That Order find
Another shape must come; or in its play
At last God's Self should die, all cast behind,
No further newness in the bounded worlds to slay
But Bound Himself, and, boundless, flow combined
With Him, all darkness, as before His Yea
Brought into life the mirroring delight
This work afforded. Knowledge burnt away.
Must He too die to Darkness, self-indict,
And cast away His Crown of circling worlds, the ray
Of vision now go out? He saw the height
Of Satan's envy touch Him. Order lay
In loss of order, and the worlds rocked in His fright.

    What was this consequence of Love, that Satan's lie
    Of merit might infect the corner stones of earth?
    What could the Father mean to give this darkness light?
    The other two of Trinity saw their dispatch.

Brought in division to engulfing doubt,
Back from the rims of thought, like ink or dye
Staining Him inward, racing the angels' rout,
He pulls Himself together in His Eye,
Sucked toward a vision of His depths, not proud
Of constancy.
                    Michaël by his chase made dry
Sucks up the waters for his fury's drought,
Unleashed in fear, and spews at Judgment grown
So brilliant it enkindles night.
                              Drawn stout
Against him, Satan fires the trembling Throne
One query: "What eternity is wrought
One moment of created Time that we should moan
Its passing?"
                    God's love gasps. Then with a shout
Michaël drives on, his hammer-force God's own,
And Satan fends him with each three-pronged lie
Of Light – that Rule, Right, Reason are the bone
Of Godhead and the flesh.
                              The hammers fly,
Beat back the tridents on their Law's unyielding stone,
Blow backed on blow, until like nails they die
In steam, plunged in the earth, where Satan's thrown
Deep in the streams of Time to scourge and crucify.

       To this stroke wars were nothing and the wave
       Of hurricanes a ripple, As the worlds shook free.
       The Triune interceded as the universe
       Grew black. And over all the end of time loomed large.

About the heavens the quivering stars blink out;
The night grows chill. Black winds race cross the sky
And wash the four-square founding stones with doubt;
Earth's firmament of brass breaks loose; one cry
And torn her bowels, all her seas ooze out
In pain beyond the firmament into the dry
Wastes men call Sheol, bitter waters out

Of sight of man. The empty spaces groan
In drought and silence, Darkness spreads throughout
Them and the mirror fades. In ice all moan
Upon the wind; all fails in fragments out
The self-punctured vision; and the worlds cease to be known.
The Brightness swallowed, God's great eye flares out.
Eternal silence infinite.
The Throne
Carnelian with the chill, empty and dry,
Cracks with its own lost weight, riv'n and blown,
Falls into Time. Dark No Thing swirls awry,
Eats up the hills, the valleys, drinks the seas, and lone
About the night soughs in its fright one sigh.
Then Dark contracts – spreads wide – a bleeding cone –
And vomits Heaven and Earth to praise a newborn I.

Love is the root of law, Love in despite.
A newborn cuddles in his mother's arms.
Suffering feeds sustenance as angels cry.

As if annealed by torment the Godheads rose
Out of the churning fours to mount the Throne;
From its riven adamant new sapphire glows.
Refracted rainbows of creation's dawn
Whirl in His blinking eyes the choric rose.
"Let be the Light!" His word. The Light of Satan shone
In matter, dark next the Life it would oppose.
"Divide the Deeps!" God's Word rejoiced. The gnome
Sank down in matter; free energy froze
Into organic life. Light filled the Dome
As Michaël laughed, for life in dying grows,
And all the waters of the worlds together foam
On farthest shores their living flows.
"Let Life be Law!"
– Satan's imperfect gnome,
Order by merit, is undone, yet sown
Life lives by Law, force rears the Dome.
The Godheads kiss. Their loves Law's stone

And freedom's fire conjoin into the fertile loam
And breathe for the Living Law a frame of bone.
The God looked out on green leaves and his home,
Grasped with His firm new fingers earth, and breathed alone.

IV. Visions of Space and Time

V. LOVE AND MARRIAGE

ANNIVERSARY THOUGHTS

What say for love and marriage,
After more than forty years?
Still one like horse and carriage
They used to say were pairs?

Horses grow old, and carriages
Crack and turn grey in rain;
While love grows cold, and marriages
Wither under strain.

But somewhere in the faithful heart
The coals of joy burn blue,
And when love cools, remembered art
Rekindles what we knew.

For marriage is the lover's art
Of answering when bid,
And she, my long love, for her part,
Knows where my heart is hid.

TWILIGHT

Were we then whirled in Fææërie?
A dream scene in our eye?
And did the hills then truly sing
And leap up in the sky?

There on the ridge-top safe and high
We played old music on our pipe
And laughed the years gone by.

It was another world we stood,
Another stone beneath,
And in your hand my heartbeat could
Be stilled by but one breath.

It was a marvel, never met again;
It was a blink, an angel's wipe
Of wing across our faces. Then . . .

AT THE LILLY POOL

We're in disguise,
      this fancy-dress,
only the eyes
      betray the rest;
no one must know,
      just you and me,
wrapped in these rags
      of infirmity.
But when the door's locked,
      shades closed and down,
deep in my mind's blocked
      recall and frown,
there you, without disguise,
      wait by the pool,
moonsilver'd, Artemis,
      and I your fool.

BY THE FORTIETH YEAR

Does marriage in the fortieth year begin
to prophesy? To vision futures intertwined
With fabric of our fears and daily sin?

Four decades living two as one inclined
stores up a mighty past of memories
so bright it leaves the present blind,

Sight leaves the heart no room but reveries
of "country service," sand piles, hot red clay,
your hands tomatoed, canning litanies –

Stored up in albums, pictures of the day,
of sopping Sunday dresses, tar-soaked shoes,
your smile in moonlight –
                                    Almost I must pray.

Recall! A garden made the evening's news
rehearsed from mutual workdays told in bed –
Birthday candles – to what secret are these clues?
What have we witnessed? What refused?

MY SON, BENJAMIN, TERROR OF TURTLES

So patiently amid the shallows,
  he stalks frogs,
and contemplates the turtles'
  sleep on logs,
then in the cusp of evening
  through the dark
he chases blinks of fireflies, laughing,
  for their spark.
My little savant, teacher, this my son,
Instructs in wonder at the treasures won.
The mystery of life, its forms,   intricacies,
why wild things live or die by strife
  and some tastes please,
The plenitude of life, God's mysteries,
All creatures of delight, is what he sees.
And I, his senior, father,
  would-be friend,
Can only marvel at how stories end.

THE CIRCLE OF THE CAMPFIRE

Darkness surrounds the happy heart as night
Contracts the circle and the hearthfires die.
It is a realm of calm, of quiet sky,
Massing shadows and far ponderous height
Admitting only wind and air and flight
Of fantasies between the mind and eye;
All forms, all bounds, all definitions fly
Before the universal loss of sight.

Not cruel, darkness comforts with the hint
Of comprehension, uniform content;
The mind tries focusing one last intent;
Then tired with appetite, to dreamy sleep
Follows the body to the bedroll's heap,
Reft of distinction, drifting the numb deep.

JOHN, PIGGYBACK

You laughed on Daddy's shoulders when a beam
      of sunlight broke the dusk beneath the trees,
laughed us from shadow into magic dream
      where laughter's sunlight and the long run ease.
Who carried whom? Who was the longer weight?
      Lighter than light, both son and daddy ride
on light over the earth, inebriate
      of laughter, heaven in the heaving side.
Somewhere that ride goes on, tripping and tossed;
      somewhere the hills are bright, unfaded light;
we run to catch the sunbeams 'fore they're lost,
      you lifting, laughing, love into my sight.
Son carries father, father carries son.
Who then is burdened when the ride is done?

ON DISCUSSING TOLKIEN WITH MY DAUGHTER
For Helen

I heard the gull-cry echo cross the sands.
The long call of water drums the shore.
Where is the aching heart drawn now across the wave?
The western isles recede against the night.
We are now west, and east the rising sun,
Yet westerly is elf-home, as our fathers knew.
Crossing the continent entails the deserts
And the glittering halls of barbary
More dangerous than Umbar or the Lebennin.
We must escape or slip the eyes of Morgul,
We must pass other Watchers in the night.
But we have mapped for us the holy way,
The only way to cast the Ring in fire.
John Ronald Reuel held the elven light
Within a tale of epic majesty.
To perdure to the end, to let it go,
Not in our will, but in the miracle
Of time, God's Providence, the unsought boon.
So shall we safely pass, and safely find our home.
This is the mystery, the spiritual sense,
The secret map of Mordor in our heart,
Following Frodo while our Aragorn
Steps on the Paths the Dead have guarded for this very hour.
Two actions, two responding hearts in one,
The mystery of journey is the path of the sun.

PROVIDENCE

"Roper, the field is won!"
St. Thomas More, to his son-in-law, on the scaffold

For Helen my daughter, on her birthday

Such confidence in Christ and in His Providence
Come but with long-tried sanctity and Grace.
But I've seen dawn break through treetops on the hills,
and slowly rouge the nightskies with the hue of hope.
I've seen small fledglings drop from nests and fly,
spring into air on wings almost too small to lift.
I have seen winter snows melt quickly off the roof,
and ice break up on lakeside with a groan.
I have seen children learn to speak and write as if
they never had rebelled against the rule.
I've seen my children flare on their destined heights,
their lights bright beacons in the nation's dark.
What then to fear from any ghost that comes?
What could negate His promised victory?
Providence reigns. And hope, unseen, defends.
There is no question from the night, no dark
that will not lift, no pain that will not turn.
All shall be well, and all shall be well, and all
behovely. As the day departs the night.
True then His line, connection of His points,
the irretraceable trajectory of God,
His Providence. "Roper, the field is won!"

THE IRIS BEDS
For Nancy, my sister

Tall they seem, purple and gold in memory,
Those flags our Hillside garden flew –
They flutter yet in the breeze of memory –
And we the children playing in the grass,
Return to peer wide-eyed and wondering,
At remembered Spring.

They flutter yet, green swords between the lines
Of dragon teeth, stones ripped from the Tennessee hills,
those iris Mother loved, flag blossoms fluttering,
purples and whites and yellows, cheering the sun each day.
her gardens ringed the outline of her house, above, below,
defining Hillside as her own domain,
declaring victory over time and dearth.

Year after year returning in their joy,
this spread of color, glad conforming with her plan,
more docile than her children, more sublime.
Yet we her children, learning from their glee,
rejoiced as well to join her gardening.

HORSE AND RIDER
My Sister Sarah and her little brother

She carried him piggy-back o'er the green grass,
And laughed at his glee as they saw the world pass,
And if she was weary, she didn't let on,
She knew then, knows now, that the joy is soon gone.
The Christ-child is rider, the horsey is you,
So ride round the garden, and meet there the true.
Now giddy-up horsey, ride fast to the fair,
Your gift is an angel's cheer, his laughter your air.

ECHOES
For Trudy, sister and friend

The lilt of Stardust, Stairway to the Stars,
An echo of the night, spills into Chopin,
Then to Grieg, Rachmaninoff – some bars
Of Brahms, then laughter, where it all began.

Sounds of the Nashville evenings linger clear.
Where did they go? Who's listening now beside
To happiness, to love, to safety there
Somewhere in memory, somewhere outside?

Another child builds towers upstairs, above
The piano's room, intent on play. And hears.
Sonatas soaring into songs of love.
That child's grown children hear and calm their fears.

What was once music now repeats in rhyme;
Always a living heart still keeping time.

V. Love and Marriage

JOSEPH – A HOLY WAY
For William Joseph

Only to nurture, care, prepare are fathers given.
Joseph the father shed our ignorance
When visions of the night announced the fact.
Toward that which opens on the altar stone
Blest Joseph turned, like us in awe, when first
He chose to take his virgin love to wife
And love what never his as his alone,
The miracle revealed on stable floor.
Only to nurture, care, prepare, are fathers given.

The dry rod blossomed with the soft hawthorne
And vision grew, a vision of the way.
Not to escape the pain, the suffering,
But to achieve the type is destiny.
The rod once flowered with a wintry spring,
Even the frantic searching temple crowds,
His last son vanished, could not rob his hope.
Only that "Father's business" struck him to the heart.
The dry rod blossomed with the soft hawthorne.

To father any son is to assent
To sacrifice. All sons are He, our lines
Illusion that we have another life
To live deeds we have missed. Our gift is care.
The Father, holding in his arm the Child,
From the concerns of carpentry is called
Away into the greater Art, the pain
Of joining for a house not his, not bone
Of his bone, flesh of flesh, but his by love.
To father any son is to assent.

GREEN DAY AND WELCOME REST
For Louise, remembering

Green crests the living hills of Harpeth,
Green in the noonday sun.
Over the ridge low cloudbanks gather,
White mountains, one on one.

It is a fair day, a festive day,
With July just begun;
And on the roof one peacock, green,
Spreads lazy azure fan.

Sleepily, wastefully, all the land
In sun's warmth, shutting down
To welcome afternoon repose.
It's rest when labor's done,

This is the rest where nature grows,
Creation's Sabbath rest
Kept daily at the hot sixth hour,
And leaving its bequest.

It is our day's hire, fair reward,
This blissfull little hour.
But is it only mortals' dream
That fills the air with power?

V. Love and Marriage

NATURAL BRIDGE

No other lovers live,
       but we renew
This muted night
       their miracle of song,

My hand above the silence
       held by yours,
Two revelers on thin air dance
       as on a bridge of stone.

TIGER FEARS

No petty accidents befall
the ordinary flow of this or that,
mere watching shadows hug the wall.

And then, as tigers, torn from our repose,
we lift wet muzzles
sniffing fearfully the gloom.

MER VOYAGE

Only the crystal certainty of wave,
In a shell rocked aimlessly before the wind,
Enchanted waters lapping without sound.

You rose, through waters clearer than the dawn,
And in one shell, we two, began
This mer-life, voyaging toward the shore.

VI. THE KING IN EXILE

EXILE

The final wonder of the wavering day
In violet shadow over summer fields,
Woodsmoke in air and haze of August dust –
A rabbit starts, scared off its evening feed,
A light breeze tossing the dark maple leaves.
Eastward, the low hills purple into night.
Oh – cruel wealth of exile, taste of home,
This August light at sunfall in the West.
It is the plenitude of sense, the abundance filled;
It is the aroma of warm earth and blowing green,
All harmonies awakened in the soul at once
That is our proof of paradise – and of
Its loss – unrealized, unreached, desired.
In every air upon the hills, the scent
Of resin, sweep of corn, the shivered heat
Down in the bottoms, and the cough and bark
Of foxes in the shadowed wood, the call
To turn back homeward with the close of day.
Exiled in beauty, castaway on wealth,
Extravagance of sense unrolled before us,
We stand sad strangers, exiled on this shore.

THE OUTER BANKS

The moon reclines this evening in her cup,
Long shadows silver and the stars still there.
And everywhere
Our stretch of sea sand lives awash in light.

There is a time for sadness in the night,
For watching ships pass by far out the Sound
And all around
To find the sorrow of high kings fallen in quest.

But not an evening where light laves the west,
Holding the motion of the turning stars,
And through our bars
Wash wave on wave of harmonies unthought.

Why then, if we may hear with ears untaught
Such music from the seas and skies,
Should the surprise
Of plenitude have left a thirsting in the cup?

THE GULLS

I've heard the Gulls call on the western shore,
and stopped my ears with music while I ran for ome.

But now they fly here to the sheltered lakes,
from easterly, along the Great Lakes road,
and make their homes among my forest trees.
Crying and crying their shrill ghostly cries.

Gulls are for gulling all unwary souls.
Weaving above us in the autumnal air,
they fly to mock us with Atlantean pride,
oceans of longing in their obscure word.

No one escapes them, no one's immune.
The echo of the waves pleads through their calls.

VI. The King in Exile

THE GREAT SECRET

Echo: All is Grace, the marvel of delight;
And Glory fires you to return to fight.

I. The Miracle that Speaks no Word
For Kate

They say that dwelling near the cataracts
Of Aswan, or Niagara, one can't hear
The thunder or the tumult, only facts,
The silent memories of sounds of fear.

Do we lose hearing, or the power of sight
For the marvelous? Kept awash in plenitude,
Immersed in color, shade, and light?
– As if the shapes rehearsed were not renewed.

Birdsong and butterflies, a sudden breeze,
The glint of sunbeam on the morning's dew,
The bass of car horns through the distant trees,
And startling – sudden knowledge – all is new.

What is the roar of mystery I have not heard?
What is the miracle that speaks no word?

II. The Fire Has Smoke

It is no wizard's trick to know you're alive;
The sameness of the moments dulls the sense.
You wake, you shave, you dress and keep pretense
Of working, so your conscience won't revive.
You smile and speak when spoken to, and drive,
Careful not to speed or hit the garden fence.
Nothing to draw attention to an expired license,
Or cause your kids to treat you like you were five.

But try as you may, one day the spell is broke,

You see, and smell, and know the fire has smoke.
The sunburn stings, the light switch sparks,
And in the closet, coats; they all are darks.
Sameness is fragile, you are not allowed
Routine, the sweet illusion of the proud.

III. To Speak the Truth

The secret is, there is no Secret, Code,
Nor Password to unlock the hidden door.
The Questor stands befuddled on the floor
And shakes his head, frustrated to explode
The gate, break down the doors, but nothing comes;
The silence at his question mocks his soul;
Nothing makes sense, nothing makes error whole,
And there the doorway that belies his sums.

Only the riddle in the ancient runes,
The tantalizing recipe, to speak,
To make known publicly how weak
His self-sought knowledge, its cramped boons.
To speak Truth, is to speak Love, agony;
Love forces doors to open, sets him free.

IV. Underneath, Underneath

Burdened with plenitude and bereft of sense,
The questing mind finds solace in its pain.
Daughter of Indolence, Despair again
Makes of the wondrous Word but case and tense.

No tongue to speak the vision glimpsed by day,
Nor voice to sing the glories of the night,
The mystery is hidden in the light
Of galaxies, of paradigms of play.

Only the knowledge that the doors are there,
That somewhere there is entry for the soul,

That underneath, the strong unyielding roll
Of being stands beneath the empty air,
Keeps the long Quest from foundering in the muck,
The knowledge that the end is not mere luck.

V. The Great Secret

All then is Grace? All mysteries?
The moonbow glinting in the drop of dew,
The birdsong starting from the gloomy yew,
The dog bark, cat's cry, from the distant trees,
Over the rooftop honking flights of geese
Heading for warmer climes, signal their clue,
And turn, great wheels, toward destinations new.
And frogs, tree frogs, peep constantly their pleas.

Everything leaps to life, is poised upon the mark;
The world awakes, the first light breaks; the heart
Thrills with awareness that it can survive.
So bearing God, like mothering the dark,
All senses ring with knowledge of the art
Of speaking, singing, shouting, "I'm alive!"

Re-echo: All is Grace, the marvel of delight;
And Glory fires you to return to fight.

MYSTERIUM RESURRECTIONIS

1. O Lady, *Mater*, if our sense be true,
   what we thought sealed in tomb is false –
   where be its earthliness? That Something New
   that rends familiarity from loss
   beggars the tawdry gowns we hide it in.
   The body's wet, we'd swear, with substances
   that can not pass beyond death's puissant power –
   Still, they his friends swore, tho' their distances
   dissolve our trust. What we tremble at this hour,
   his body ris'n from death, O *Dulcis*, from our sin.
   Mater Fidei, ora pro nobis peccatoribus,
   nunc, nunc, et in hora mortis nostrae.

2. Thus resurrection is the key, O *Dulcis*, turned
   within the lock of sense to let us home.
   It is the answer to our fears, our doubts, so burned
   within our sight that we can't roam
   the avenues of death but must find room
   for heaven all around our prison cell.
   This resurrection once proclaimed repeats each time
   we see the beauty of love's face repel
   the lie of loneliness in answered rhyme.
   So reborn love's deep foliage starts to bloom.
   Mater Fidei, ora pro nobis peccatoribus,
   Nunc et in hora timoris nostrae

3. Arisen, *Clemens*, and alive again.
   That is our hope. Yet not arisen from death,
   The final step, arisen from mortal sleep,
   The sleep of heart, sin's comfort bound to breath.
   Arisen in joy and rising every morn,
   The new life sings and beckons to its light.
   Why has this wak'ning taken so much time?
   This understanding poised upon the heights,
   Been granted only after so much pain?

Is it the desert where the soul is born?
Pro peccatoribus, O Mater, ora nunc
Et in hora mortis nostrae

VI. The King in Exile

DAWN ON LATERAN
Montini Prepares His Answer

(A dramatic monologue with voices)

"A faltering dawn on Lateran leaves night;
Who serve with me this morning God's own Son
Assemble with the Slave of Slaves, the might
Of all this age's opposition
To the pervasive lie. The failing sight
Of age, the stiffened knees, this paltry few, are spun
With multitudes, the unseen cloud alight.

"Only the hands move over bread and wine,
But Power broods the abyss of wrong and right.
Heart-breaking manual acts of the Pope entwine
The shadowed substance in our mortal plight.
But mind unlike the hands quails at the design
In illo tempore.

      "Is Satan's light
Of reason reasonless, mere savorless brine
All merit? What but His submission won
Beyond the facts of flesh?" The hands incline.
Bells clang. And from the lifted Host hosts run
For love to darkness Resurrection proves divine.
Only this death illumines what is done!
Redeem our history, Good Lord, True Vine,
That this age fail not with your harvest to be one.

"For my perplexity,
In ease the ravenous gut of Merit feeds,
On generations judged unborn to die.
Named Mammon once, and Moloch, he now leads
His white-coat acolytes in litany,
Of triumph, certain now, to the new creeds.
And children pass through saline fire to glut the lie
Satan's rebellion cast over the needs
Of Nature. Merit sets the meed. His claws
Scrape at the soul. How many hidden greeds

VI. The King in Exile

Push at the mind's will, find or make a cause
To justify rebellion, hide the seeds
Of willful blindness in the casuistic clause?
To justify the avarice that breeds
New comforts for this present age and gnaws
The world-root of the Church. The Papacy
Must sanction contraception of the laws
Of nature for the Natural Man? Must try
Accommodation with the Rational Lie that draws
To trial all life, mind, and history?
At axle of the worlds, the Popes must pause
From manual labor to debate how best to die?

"What then my dilemma?
Beyond the intersection of two times,
Reft, by their heresy, of home they fly
Back over sundering seas to heathen climes.
Theirs is no simple death of beasts to die,
These apostates, but torment in their crimes
Erases even gratitude from memory.
They scorn their heritage, the paradigms
Of virtue manifest in all the saints.
All of this lust for license, craving, climbs
Into the fold as we relax constraints.
It is God's law in wedlock that sublimes
The appetites; thus holy heritage attaints
Their argument, who would infect our times
With pagan nightmare, of the coward's plaints.
he strong need no incentive alibi;
The married laity knows God's restraints
As chastity and perfect love. Our eye
Must be the shepherd's, guarding them from Satan's feints
Lest thief-like, heresy pretend to gratify
Their lust, and nature in them faithless faints.
What but God's Will in wedlock must we glorify?

"I hear my experts, sure of truth:
'We lie between two armies, that of right
And that of all our sentiment and sense of past.
Right asks of us to recognize the layman's plight

That marriage and his married love may last
Only in the recognition of his sexual delight.
His stifling of response, the imposed task,
Stifles his love. And where the might
Of Church denies his love, man will rebel,
And leave the Church behind, to follow inner light.'

'The force of history, the times, impel
Us to redraw, to change what we have thought the right
And modernize the rule to match the age's swell.'

'Behind statistics or the recondite
Theologies of Natural Law we sell —
This simple truth — we will be passed
By history, grow obsolete and fell
And lose authority to Time, outcast.
The church that will survive will break its outgrown shell
And champion liberty the greatest Grace amassed
By all her saints through time! Hear, then, the knell
Of the unreasonable swell through ages vast.'

How, then, shall the Pope reply?
What thing is human life without God's Will?
Where is there enclave from entropy for man
Within the churning of Time's monstrous mill?
Submission to Creation and the darkened plan,
The sight of Him who broke the Deep like steel,
Can not be reasonable Law, not stone, not ban,
But coinherent joy. And in our cell
Of light the reasonable proves seldom God
For never more than reason, free from will.
What seems the timely way, reason's best rod,
Betrays us, willingly, to glut our fill
On others for our own delight, thinking our god
s God.

     "So Adam, on the sacred hill
Plucked power for the future's sake – one pod
Of knowledge and his progeny would stand
As gods among the stars, no more to plod

About the garden of this earth mere men.
Did Pius so, my predecessor, with one nod
To save the Church, one the perfidious clan
Of Chosen, choose the Church – as if we trod
Some other road than His, fed from some other Hand?

"And I the *Servus Servorum Dei*:
So small a thing, with hardly any voice
Nor strength to stay the clashing mills of Law,
This tiny thing, this weak thing, a man's choice.
In this sole glory one man's life may gnaw
The universe of death 'til it destroys
Destruction, or transhumanizes mortal flaw
To godly resurrection. God employs
All history in any moment bound
As each to each, or each in each, as ploys,
Hooks, for His soul-fishing, mysterious round
Of victory through death. So here the poise
Of worlds is balanced in a word this world has found
Already ludicrous, has judged but noise.
Submission – to the Will, to Him. Profound,
Superfluous gift from man out of death's maw!
No, we may not choose history nor sound
Reason, no, nor specially that straw
Of false hope, Kindness. Not for these will we be drowned
With Nature in that death to which all draw.
In His love, by His hand, His Church is crowned;
And wedded life by choice shall seek God's higher Law.

"I must consider *Urbem et Orbem* –
At axle of the Worlds Eternal Rome
Sleeps in the tranquil eye of sacrament.
All of the saintly host turn toward their home
And seek the dancing of the firmament,
Leaving us here alone in the drafty dome.
Appetite feeds on Appetite and element
Wars with element deep in the gloam
Of history, all moments revenant.
The Emperor is tombed. The silent dome
Of Heaven mocks his multitudinous fall.

Over the demes of empire demons roam.
Only the papal hands uplift left to forestall
The barb'rous horde and tend the hearth of Rome.
Only the hands to break or bless. The brawl
Of headless members is the monument
The rule of merit built us. The breasts of Gaul
Are sour and stone the womb of Orient.
Only the hands uplifted beyond Law recall
The Acts of Plenitude, bridge ruinment
Of Empire with the Redemptoral Fall.
The tranquil sleep of men is shored in Sacrament.

"*Ite, Missa Est.* I can foresee my epitaph.
Beyond the human, beyond Law and Fate
Lies mystery, Love infinite, desire.
The mystery of suffering hides the gate
Of Heav'n, Exchange of fire for fire.
All moments one, the agony, the wait,
The Judgment, Resurrection, and ascending gyre.
Praise to the hands, forgot in the debate,
That break the bread of sacrifice each day.
Their constant vigil stirs the Enemy's hate.
Praise to the valor steadfast in the fray,
Resolve grown harder, hope grown desolate.
Heart must grow keener, courage the colder, mood more fey.
Over the roofs of Rome clouds convocate;
Must Paul, *Servus Servorum,* but note and turn away,
His task now done? Christ's body feeds His byre.

"Truth has been spoken, though it cost what may.
And cost the Church it shall, what the Law require.
Most reasonable error still shall reason pay.
It is in mystery man collects his hire,
Order by order, merit massed in play,
And glory burst from hiding in the night's desire."

GOODBYE, GOODBYE
(After reading R. L. Stevenson's "Farewell to the Farm")

O rest your head, my sleepy babe,
Rest your bright head on my shoulders.
We've raced the day past hill and dale,
Jumped fallen trees, climbed boulders.

And you, my son, my light, my joy,
Sang me the paths and orders;
Now rest your head, my golden boy,
And bless these darkling borders.

Through woods and glades, down hillside stairs,
Between blue shadows massing,
The fox kits in their twilight lairs
Must marvel at our passing.

Sing! Sing, my sunshine, gentle tune,
The wordless songs of heaven,
The ooh-ooh-ah beneath the moon
Of sleepy babes of even.

I hold, I hold you, safe at rest,
My feet made light in yearning;
And with no stumble still be blessed
Up to our door returning.

Goodbye, goodbye, to everything.
To tree, to stone, to laughter;
Goodbye, goodbye, to babes that sing,
And blessed be what comes after.

ACKNOWLEDGMENTS

The poems of Part One, Flags, first appeared in a chapbook entitled *Flags and Other Poems*, published by Allen Press, 1963. The poems, "The Cast of Valor," "The Primal Lie," and Dawn on Lateran," first appeared as parts of *War in Heaven*, also published by Allen Press, 1973. They are all reprinted with the kind permission of Robert M. Allen.

The poem, "The Outer Banks" was published in *Raleigh Poetry, The Seventies, Special Issue, 1972, Southern Poetry Review,* under the title "The Krater." The section of "Cast of Valor, Hood in Georgia," was published in another Special Edition of *Southern Poetry Review, North Carolina Poetry, The Seventies* (1975)

The poem "The Permanence of Space," appeared in *The Sewanee Review* (Autumn, 1972). The poem 'Farewell, My Father" appeared under the title "Elegy for an Old Ghost" in *The Sewanee Review* (October-December, 1964).

Rollin A. Lasseter

Rollin A. Lasseter retired in 2003 from the English faculty of the University of Dallas. He graduated *Summa Cum Laude* from Vanderbilt University, and attended Yale University as a Woodrow Wilson Fellow, where he received his M.A. and Ph.D. His dissertation was on W.B. Yeats. He was Director of the Honors Program at the University of Kentucky, where he received the Great Teacher Award twice. He was given tenure in the English Department at North Carolina State University. He did post-graduate work at the University of Notre Dame, and taught at St. Mary's College, South Bend, and Indiana University at South Bend before joining the English faculty in 1992 at the University of Dallas. He converted to the Catholic Faith in 1980.

Lasseter designed a program for teaching poetry and composition for high school students which is now used in several private and parochial schools. For several years he taught Latin, Ancient History and Literature, and English Composition at a classical curriculum secondary school, Trinity School at Greenlawn, which his six children attended. He was Director of Curriculum at an independent Catholic school and continues as a consultant for curriculum. He is currently general editor and primary writer for a series of history textbooks for junior high and high school students, the Catholic Schools Textbook Project

His poetry has won several awards over the years, though this volume is the first published verse for several years now.